PSYCHOTHERAPY AND PROCESS: THE FUNDAMENTALS OF AN EXISTENTIAL-HUMANISTIC APPROACH

James F. T. Bugental, Ph.D.
Private Practice, San Rafael, California
Home Faculty, Humanistic Psychology Institute

ADDISON-WESLEY
PUBLISHING COMPANY
Reading, Massachusetts
Menlo Park, California
London • Amsterdam
Don Mills, Ontario • Sydney

For Karen Marie Bugental

This book is in the
ADDISON-WESLEY SERIES
IN CLINICAL AND PROFESSIONAL
PSYCHOLOGY

Leonard D. Goodstein
Series Editor

 Printed in the United States of America. Published simultaneously in Canada. Library of Congress Catalog Card No. 77-83031.

ISBN 0-201-00333-3
BCDEFGHIJK-DO-79

Preface

Prologue to a Journey: A Perspective for an Existential-Humanistic Psychotherapy

Psychotherapy is a *trip*, especially psychotherapy such as this book describes. The word "trip" has many meanings. One meaning of the word "trip" is "an emotional adventure"—psychotherapy is an emotional adventure. Another meaning of the word "trip" is "a journey, a going from one place to another" —psychotherapy is also a journey.

The psychotherapy journey is in some ways similar to the seventeenth century ventures of those who pulled loose from their European homes to risk the voyage across the Atlantic in search of new lives in America. They did not have any sure knowledge of how much they were leaving or what they would find. Many had found the old ways of being intolerable, and all hoped the New World would give them something better. Once they had made the journey, there was no true going back possible. It was a one-way trip—just as life and intensive psychotherapy are one-way trips.

In these pages I'm going to describe a journey: the general plan of the trip; the two people who will travel together; what they will bring to their departure; the maps which will guide them (and which they hope are reasonably accurate); the vessel which they will trust to carry them; the roles each must play in the crossing, the destination they seek and the one they find; the new journeying that arrival opens up; and finally the personal experience of the therapist who is the guide on the trip.

What does it mean to be alive? What is the fundamental principle or characteristic of human life? What distinguishes human life from other life forms?

To be alive is to be able to do things, to see and hear what's going on, to move, to taste, to smell, to touch, and to feel emotions. To be alive is to be aware of colors and sounds and people and buildings and streets and grass. . . . To be alive is to think about yesterday and tomorrow and today, to be concerned about what does and doesn't happen in one's experience, to feel for others, to know love and hate and joy and sorrow and hope and envy. . . . To be alive is to be puzzled about what it means to be alive.

Life is awareness. That's the bottom line, in my opinion. I say that as person and as psychologist—especially as a psychologist with an existential and humanistic perspective. If no awareness exists or is likely to exist, that is death. Awareness is, of course, a tremendous spectrum of experience. The sunflower is *aware* of the sun, and the spiritual master is *aware* of the pure light of being—and perhaps the sunflower and the spiritual master are brothers in some ultimate way. Say rather that they are cousins, for there has been a branching in their family tree. The sunflower—so far as we know—took the route of nonconsciousness, the master that of seeking transcendent consciousness.

Life is awareness. When we go through all of the characterizations, descriptions, and careful hypotheses, it seems to me that the least common denominator is awareness. *Human life is consciousness.* Consciousness means more than choiceless awareness such as that of the sunflower—a mechanical and unselective response to an outside force. Human life is conscious life, is life conscious of itself, is awareness of a qualitatively different kind.

Human life is consciousness, and psychotherapy is the art, science, and practice of studying the nature of consciousness and of what may reduce it or facilitate it. Psychotherapy is concern with the life and death of human potentialities.

Psychotherapy is one way the living may fight for their lives while they're still alive. There are other ways such as personal determination joined to insight, religious or philosophical conversion, a really powerful friendship or love, a major life climax or tragedy, prolonged and powerful meditation or similar discipline—these are some of the other ways the living fight the death that consumes us from within. These are some of the ways the living may claim more of the life that awaits those who will take hold of it.

When we come to face how much aliveness is potential within us and how much we let slide into the death of half-awareness, we may go into a panic, or drop-out and take up yoga, or break up our marriages, or quit our jobs, or join the Moonies, or leave them. Or we may redouble our efforts—conscious and unconscious—to silence that troubling recognition of half death. Or we may go into psychotherapy.

In this book I will be describing a kind of psychotherapy that is centered on the fact of being alive, that seeks to heighten consciousness, and that tries to work with the fundamental life process of awareness as its main means for bringing to the client the possibilities for richer and more meaningful living. The basic theory of this psychotherapy is called *existential* because it has to do with the fact of existence. The value orientation of this psychotherapy is called *humanistic* because it sees the greater realization of the potentials of human beings as the most desirable outcome of the therapeutic work.

This book is written for those readers who want to be introduced to intensive psychotherapy that is neither behavioristic nor psychoanalytic. I have attempted to sketch a coherent conception of the psychological features of such work, the nature of the main procedures, and the hoped for outcomes. I have also tried to provide the reader with some sense of the subjective experience of being a client in such psychotherapy and of the experience of the psychotherapist as well.

This book may be thought of as extending the conception of psychotherapy, which I presented for professionals in *The Search for Authenticity: An Existential-Analytic Approach to Psychotherapy* (1965) and illustrated for all readers through extended case "dialogues" in *The Search for Existential Identity: Patient-Therapist Dialogues in Humanistic Psychotherapy* (1976).

San Rafael, California J.F.T.B.
January 1978

Acknowledgments

It is so manifestly impossible to recognize all who contribute to such a work as this that I will simply say "Thank you" to my clients, who are my principal teachers; to my friends and colleagues, who have given me support and counsel; and to my students, who are helping me clarify and refine my ideas and make explicit my procedures.

Special recognition also needs to be given Dr. Roger N. Walsh, whose insightful account of his own experience in this therapy (1976) has been a great gift and has enriched the chapter on therapeutic outcomes. Similarly, Dr. John F. Cogswell has made available both a published account (1971) and a specially prepared description of his experience in therapy, both of which have added to the pages which follow. Others who have contributed in various and particularly meaningful ways are G. Rogers Carrington, Dr. Robert S. Hoffman, John Levy, and Dr. Sylvia A. Tufenkjian-Mirabella. Katie Whitten deserves my very special thanks for her patience and support in the many details of readying this manuscript.

Finally, I find so much pleasure in recognizing the existential and humanistic and very personal support of my wife, colleague, companion, and buddy, Elizabeth Keber Bugental, Ph.D.

San Rafael, California
12 May 1977

James F. T. Bugental

Foreword

Clinical psychology is a rapidly expanding area of inquiry and practice. Traditional lines between clinical and the other subdisciplines of psychology are rapidly eroding. Research in information processing has direct impact upon behavior therapy, work in physiological psychology affects our work in biofeedback, community psychologists need to keep abreast of what is happening in social psychology, and so on. At the same time, clinical psychologists are being called on to work in a variety of new settings, and to continually develop new skills as well as utilize their existing skills. Health Maintenance organizations (HMOs) ask clinical psychologists not only to provide direct clinical service to clients but also to help change the health-related behaviors of clients who do not require direct service. Community mental health centers ask their clinicians to provide direct service and to assist in developing prevention programs and program evaluation procedures. These are but a few examples of how the field of clinical psychology is expanding.

It is difficult for the professional practitioner as well as the student of clinical psychology to keep in touch with what is happening in the field. Traditional textbooks can give only superficial coverage to these recent changes and the journal literature does not provide a broad overview. The Addison-Wesley Series in Clinical and Professional Psychology is an effort to fill this gap. Taken as a whole, the series could be used as an introduction to the field of clinical psychology. A subset of these books, such as those on therapy, for example, could serve as a text for a course in therapy. Single volumes can be used for seminars when supplemented by journal articles, or as supplemental texts for courses in which the instructor feels the text is lacking in coverage of that area, or for short courses for the active professional. We hope that each of these volumes, written or edited by an expert in the area, will also serve as an up-to-date overview of that area for the interested professional who feels in need of updating.

In this volume James F. T. Bugental has provided a succinct and comprehensive overview of existential-humanistic psychotherapy. All too many authors writing out of this perspective are either too philosophical or too convoluted to help the reader comprehend how this position differs from other approaches to psychotherapy. Bugental succeeds where others have failed in providing a readable and a personal statement of this often-misunderstood position.

Leonard D. Goodstein

Contents

1

The Prospect of a Journey: A Scale of Psychotherapeutic Goals

The first stage of any journey occurs in the minds of those who will eventually make the trip. Before anything else, they must have a vision of where it is they want to go and how they will get there. The travelers listen to accounts of others who have journeyed before them; they talk to those who would guide them; they read descriptions of the place they dream of; and they begin to ready themselves in subtle ways for the first actual step—the decision to go.

I will describe the kind of therapy with which this book deals, showing how it is similar to and differs from other approaches to helping people change the experience of their lives. I'll do this by setting forth a range of possible goals for therapy—a span from helping the client to be more comfortable to a total reconception of the nature of one's identity.

An existential psychotherapy is one concerned with existence, with the basic fact of being. Being is a process, and the kind of therapy with which this book deals centers around the processes of the client's life, the processes by which the client may change, and the underlying process which is life itself.

Reading about psychotherapy these days, you are apt to be overwhelmed by the great number of services which are offered. Psychoanalysis, Gestalt, transactional analysis, psychosynthesis, existentialism, bioenergetics, humanistic, Reichian, Jungian, Adlerian, primal, actualizing, and so on.

To distinguish the existential-humanistic approach, which is the subject of the book you're reading, I'll develop a scale of six levels of goals for psychotherapeutic work. Then I can identify the present perspective's place among these.

Deficiency Levels of Therapeutic Goals

Adjustment

When I put my glasses on and off my nose carelessly the frames get bent, and after a bit they hurt my ears or start listing to one side or the other. Then I take them to an optician who readjusts them. An important form of counseling serves a similar function of trying to help the client change some specific sources of discomfort in order to become better adjusted. There is a tendency to look on such work as inferior, as chiefly seeking to bring about smooth conformity to a sick society. It certainly can be a way of reducing stress for a person at odds with the environment, and that is a very appropriate goal at times for some people in some circumstances—e.g., limited funds for professional help, counselors who know their own limits and are not prepared to go into deeper work, clients whose life circumstances make it impossible to undertake more, and clients who for their own reasons want no more.

Adjustment counseling serves a very legitimate human need—to reduce pain, anxiety, conflict, or preoccupation with blame. It is concerned with symptoms, to be sure, but only those who are not carrying the burden of such symptoms can be cavalier about them.

Its purpose is to help the client understand in a practical way that much distress is self-caused. It focuses on ways the client may change habits to accommodate to the contingencies of the environment or of well-being (e.g., by stopping smoking). *Behavior modification techniques* are the epitome of this level, where they are often useful.

To be sure, we must recognize that many of the distresses of life arise from patterns more deeply ingrained in the client's makeup than will yield to adjustive counseling. There is always the possibility that the distress is signaling an underlying mode of being that will persist and bring about other difficulties if the particular symptom pattern is displaced.

> Art, a 30-year-old man, suffered repeated anxiety episodes whenever he had to speak before small groups in his work. Since this was an essential part of his job, he sought help.
>
> Counseling was largely successful in helping him speak in such situations without disabling distress. However, within three months of attaining this outcome, the client returned to the counselor complaining of an inability to concentrate or remember things at work. He was referred for more intensive psychotherapy, and at some length worked through his great fears of being invisible, of being caught up in the "machine" of his work, and of not being a person or an individual. His symptoms had signaled his fear, and simple adjustment aid did not relieve that fear.
>
> On the other hand, Betty, a twenty-two-year-old wife and mother of one child sought counseling for a complaint that was superficially very similar: She couldn't make friends with her neighbors and felt uneasy when her husband brought people home from his work. Counseling helped her recognize that she was imposing perfectionist standards on herself, trying to be the faultless homemaker. At last report, she had found new comfort in being with others, and the problem had not returned.

Gordon Allport (1937) pointed out (pp. 191–207) that some patterns of behavior become *functionally autonomous*. By this term he meant that while a habit pattern always grows out of a motivational soil as a response to some need of the person, as time passes that need may no longer exist or it may become relatively unimportant; yet the habit pattern tends to go on of its own accord.

The perfectionist young wife had always tried to please her parents by doing everything just right; unthinkingly she continued that behavior in her adult life. But no longer was it truly necessary, and she had enough gratifications and support in other areas of her life—especially in her relation with her understanding and appreciative husband—that she could relinquish that pattern. She always maintained a more than usually neat house, but the anxiety when it was not immaculate was materially reduced.

Increased Coping Efficiency

Adjustment counseling helps the client deal with situational distresses by adapting more successfully to environmental demands. A second level is identifiable in which the effort would be to help the person learn improved skills in relating with the environment, thus bringing about changed responses from it. Of course, this is an oversimplification of what actually occurs. *Coping counseling* very often focuses around examinations of major areas of the client's life—family, work, friends—with a view to disclosing recurring patterns, which bring unwanted experiences. Some examples will make this more understandable.

Hank, at age 19, was one of the youngest supervisors in his firm. He was constantly having problems getting his men to cooperate, and he was afraid he'd lose his advancement. Counseling brought him to see how his anxiety made it hard for him to *hear* his employees adequately. He was so anxious to show that he was "on top of things" that he scarcely listened before issuing orders or plunging into action.

Dora sought counseling because she thought she was sliding into alcoholism. Living alone after a traumatic divorce, she had few friends. The counselor helped her recognize how her fears of relating were carried over inappropriately from her divorce. Dora, with the counselor's support experimented with new activities and relationships and found she didn't need to fill her free time with so much drinking.

Some group therapy, encounter groups, family and marital therapy efforts are chiefly directed toward this level of therapeutic goals. The group is an exceptionally useful vehicle for counseling efforts aimed at increasing *coping effectiveness*, since the repetitive patterns which bring the client difficulty are often enacted in a group setting. Also the group usefully stimulates the same sorts of expectations of one's self and others that may be the source of repeated frustration and unhappiness—for example, the often unfounded belief that others have less difficulty in their marriages or in raising their children with the resulting guilt for failing in these regards. This is sometimes called *pluralistic ignorance*—so many people feel distress about having problems that nearly all of us share. The group is ideally suited to dispel such ignorance and with it the pain of those who feel deficient in relations with their fellows.

"Self" Renewal

I use the word "self" to refer to a person's composite image of who/what one is. It usually includes, among other things, an image of oneself in relation to family, work, friends, and so on. It contains the person's assessment of the self's strengths and weaknesses, of personal traits, of what is valued and what is feared. A person's self grows by accretion over the years and may seldom really be examined to see whether it is up-to-date and truly representative. Yet, again and again, we make choices that profoundly influence our lives in terms of this implicit image.

An important therapeutic goal is to help the person make conscious and explicit a great deal of this image of self. In the process, it is often the case that the client comes to realize that appreciable portions are truly outdated or unnecessarily constricting. The self-concept can then be modified and made far more functional and realistic. Some typical issues which concern therapy at this level have to do with the client's beliefs about what is possible in the life situation and what can be required of others in one's life, and attitudes toward oneself (self-devaluing, self-hating, or otherwise being at odds with one's being). Psychotherapy at this level seeks to help the client be more realistic, more accepting of self and others, and more able to use powers which one employs only partially. Its main goal is reduction of self-alienation, one of the most frequent destructive influences in many people in our culture.

Some typical products of this level of therapy are the following:

Ed comes to realize that he is trying to live up to an image of himself as always being a winner, the first in his group. He modifies this image and reduces the unrealistic pressure he has been putting on himself.

Flo saw herself as awkward and ungainly with men, based on several humiliating experiences in early high school days. Today she has been going from one man to another in marriages and affairs, never finding fulfillment. As soon as she wins one man, he is proven unworthy by his very acceptance of her, and Flo has to move on to another. Therapy helps her to revise her self-image and realize that she is indeed attractive today and that she need not endlessly struggle against the old picture of herself.

Being Levels of Therapeutic Growth Goals

Abraham Maslow, one of the major contributors to the development of the humanistic viewpoint in psychology, repeatedly called our attention to an important distinction in human experience. On the one hand, he pointed out, we share with all living organisms the motivating effects of deficiencies. When we lack food, water, or protection from the elements, or have similar biologic needs, we are impelled to action to correct the condition from which we suffer. On the other hand, however, human beings also are motivated by the potentialities of growth itself. We feel the incentive to make actual that which we feel is latent within us. Maslow (1968) contrasted *deficiency motivation* and *growth motivation,* and here I'll follow his model.

Adjustment and coping counseling efforts, as well as what I have termed self-renewal therapy, are chiefly concerned with deficiency motivation. They are concerned with reducing negative experiences; essentially they seek to repair one's way of being in the world. In contrast, growth, emancipation, and transcendence are goals which are concerned with realizing more from one's being. They do not seek to return the person to some presumed better, former condition so much as to draw one forward to richness and meaningfulness in life, greater than that person has known before.

This book is chiefly concerned with the growth dimensions and with the therapeutic means toward such goals. Accordingly, I will talk very little more about the first three levels of our scale, and I will spend a great deal of time on the last three.

These growth levels include many of the goals of the preceding three as they seek to reduce personal distress, but they do not stop there. They differ from the deficiency levels in their emphasis on helping clients enrich their living by opening up areas of inner and outer experience which have been closed—and often never previously sensed as possible. In many ways the term "therapy" with its implications of medical and surgical correction of illnesses and injuries is not accurate for these three levels of work. They can be called educative better than therapeutic—at least in the later stages when the truly remedial phase is past. For myself, I prefer the term "evocation"—literally, a calling forth.

> We have inherited a language that is wedded to concepts and traditions. Thus the word "psychotherapy"—originally meaning the nurturing or care of the breath or of the spirit (soul)—has come to be linked to modern medical practice. The practitioner is called *doctor,* a rather happier tradition, meaning one who teaches but still implying the activity residing in the practitioner. The associate in the enterprise has been called the *patient*—that is, one who suffers or endures. By extension this word has come to suggest passivity, and in that way it is at odds completely with the orientation of the therapy in this book. Thus we will use the awkward but serviceable term *client*—one who hears—and suggests that at least this puts the crucial action, the hearing (within oneself), back where it belongs.

Growth in Personal and Interpersonal Actualization

In the process of our development from infancy to adulthood, we each work out ways of surviving in the world, of avoiding harm as much as possible, and of getting some satisfactions. These ways become the structure of our lives; they are importantly part of how we see our own identities and how we believe the world to be. They include much that is sufficiently effective that it has stood the test of the years, but they include also much that is constricting, conflict producing, and outgrown. We try, unwittingly, to live out a child's view of life and, when we are adults, we find many inaccuracies and needless limitations within it.

These patterns or structures of our living, when viewed as ways of holding off what seems to be unbearable anxiety are called *resis-*

tances—that is, they resist what seems to be too much pain, fear, or dread. These resistances also keep from consciousness the impulses, perceptions, and emotions that are linked to those threats. Thus the resistances operate to block free and open self-exploration and internal communication in the psychotherapeutic process itself.

Genuine growth in personal and interpersonal competence, in life richness, in the unfolding of previously constricted potentialities requires that the more constricting resistances be worked through. This is a demanding and extensive process of identifying how those resistances are brought into play right in the therapeutic hour. As they are identified, the client has a new opportunity to experience what the resistances held back and what their costs are today. This is no dispassionate, evaluative process. It is an agonizing and conflictful struggle, for as the resistances are exposed and begin to be loosened, the threatening materials which they covered press into consciousness. The client is flooded with feelings of fright, pain, guilt, shame, dread, and futility, and these may mount to a point at which the client feels unable to endure letting go of the ways which for so long gave a measure of protection.

Yet the vision of what might be a less constricted way of life is powerful also, and it draws the client on to relinquish some of the old ways. Now it becomes evident that there are two kinds of resistances: One kind of resistance deals with issues that are no longer so potent in the client's life—for example, the feeling that estrangement from the parents is tantamount to death (which was true for the small child, but is not true for the adult); the fear that one will be eternally damned for being sexual; or the dread of being totally unproductive if not spurred by authorities. The other kind of resistances seeks to stem anxieties, which are as great today as they ever have been. Generally these are what may be termed existential anxieties: the fear of death, of contingency, of responsibility, of separateness, of the emptiness of the universe (Bugental, 1965, pp. 282–315).

The client may find it possible to face and work through the first type of resistances, those chiefly surviving from the past. Doing so results in relief and the release of energies long bound up in holding the repressions in place. For some clients this marks the end of a satisfactory therapeutic experience. The anxieties about which we can do nothing are shoved back into the keeping of the resistances, and therapy ends. Although this constitutes less than a complete therapeutic product, it needs to be recognized that *completeness* is always a relative matter. No form of therapy produces people truly free of resistances or repressions. Claims to the contrary are evidences of either naivete or too little appreciation of the depths of human beings.

This level does represent the achievement of some very real therapeutic gains. The client finds an increase in the feeling or potency in life as a great deal more of the center of being is taken into one's self and rescued from dependence on the opinions of others or the achievements one piles up. Often the client is moved to make changes in work, in family situation, or in life activities. For this reason, therapists working at this level frequently encourage the client's life-partner to have some parallel experience—personal therapy, an encounter group, collateral interviews, guided reading—so that there is less likelihood that the relationship of client and partner will be a casualty of therapy.

Despised image

A frequent gain at this level is the exposure and release of what Karen Horney (1950) calls the *despised image* of the self. This is the feared conception of what one might be found out to be if all disguise were pulled away. It is an unrealistically repugnant image spawned of all the hidden, shameful secrets and derogations of a lifetime. Successful therapy at the growth level often leads to the exorcising of this inner demon.

Existential Emancipation

This level picks up where the preceding one leaves off. The confrontation with existential anxiety—the anxiety that arises from the conditions of life itself—is made as unblinkingly as client and therapist can endure, which is always something less than fully. Nevertheless the exposure of the resistances goes forward, and the pursuit of full and unhampered inner awareness is continued.

Slowly, if client and therapist persist, there emerges a fresh vision of how life might be with most constraints relaxed. Then there comes a time of crisis for most who venture this far. Now the client must face the possibility of genuinely relinquishing the old ways of being, ways which are integrated into the very fabric of personal identity and the world in which that identity is set. Now the client has the possibility of moving into a truly new way of being. This possible new living is, in its deepest significances, radically different from any previous level. Rather than repairing and bringing the self up to date or even developing a new self, now the possibility opens of breaking free of full identification with the self in any importantly limiting way.

Such a freeing from the self is a goal which only a few years ago would have seemed the wildest fantasy. Today the evidence for this possibility is accumulating from the reports of psychedelic studies, of altered states of consciousness, of peak experiences, of anthropological accounts, of spiritual teachers, and of the findings of depth psychotherapists and their patients. The self, we are coming to realize, is a construct of our consciousness. It is arbitrary, not a constitutional given. Its particular content and form are occasioned by the experience of one's life but are in no sense immutable.

Indeed, and this is the key point, one need not be identified with one particular self-configuration. One may be able to accept a way of being in the world (a self), which is appropriate to the life situation, but set it aside on occasion and to some extent. This sounds very far out to most of us, and it certainly is well beyond the conceptions of our nature on which we were raised. I am not going to elaborate on the idea here, but I will return to it in Chapter 8 and try to make clearer just what therapy may help some people to do.

Idealized image

Getting free of identification with the self is furthered as the *idealized image* (which is the reverse of the despised image described at the previous level) is laid bare and relinquished. This hidden, often quite grandiose, conception of what one might be *if only* circumstances favored is as much a destructive influence as is its darker twin. It paralyzes effort because every action is certain to fall short of the exaggerated model. No achievement can really satisfy no matter how well performed. Yet the client fights letting go of this near-devine, but cancerous, ideal as though giving up a cherished promise.

Transcendence

I cannot write about the transcendent level of personal evolution from any extent of personal experience. I have visited the shores of this new world at times, indeed made some expeditions inland; yet I am by no means a pioneer and far from being a settler. Still I have been privileged to accompany some who have ventured deeper and stayed longer than I. To be sure, no one I know can yet take up residence there—all visit, explore, and return. It is from such reports and from my own all too limited excursions that I write.

Psychotherapy is only one possible route to this new world; others include religion, meditation, psychedelics, and self-transcending service. Psychotherapy is the route I know best, and it is the basis of my report here.

A core meaning of the term "transcendence" is "going beyond"—going beyond, in particular, the dichotomies which we unthinkingly accept as the givens of our lives: good/bad, right/wrong, real/unreal, I/other, health/illness, growth/decline, life/death, God/human. It is not that we discard these comparisons, but that they are seen in a more inclusive perspective. Imagine primitives who have lived their lives through in a mountain valley, hearing from time to time about a great water extending as far as the eye can see. They would scarcely think that possible until one day they are taken up in an airplane so that they can see their village in the valley, the mountain, *and* the distant ocean. No longer is it either/or in their world; so it may become both and in ours. We know this as an abstraction, but in transcendence we know it in being. Maslow (1971) pointed to the many meanings of transcendence in describing the farther reaches of human potential.

We talk of "seeing," as does Castaneda (1974), with new meaning, expressing our growing recognition that the world is—as is the self—a construction as much as a discovery of consciousness. Thus those who persevere for the transpersonal journey experience in their own innerness that space and time may melt like a Dali watch, that we live in but one plane—and that an arbitrary one—while other possibilities surround us all the time.

Summary

Table 1.1 sets forth some of the dimensions I've discussed above and some others to recapitulate the similarities and differences among these six levels of therapeutic goals. One must not regard these as too firmly fixed or too clearly distinguished from one

Table 1.1 Comparisons among six levels of psychotherapy goals.

Category	Deficiency Motivation				Growth Motivation	
	Counseling		Therapy		Evocation	
	Adjustment	Coping	Renewal	Growth	Emancipation	Transcendence
Mental realm	Conscious	Conscious and preconscious	Preconscious	Preconscious and unconscious	Unconscious	Inner vision
Focus of attention	Content	Content	Content more than process	Process more than content	Process	Inner search
Reality assumption	Consensus self-and-world concept	Consensus self-and-world concept	Same but some self change	Reconstructed self-and-world concept	Fluid self-and-world concept	Nonattachment
Goals	Change behavior to fit world demands	Develop skills to interact with world	Replacing nonfunctional self-percepts	Life reorganization and revitalizing	Freeing from "self"-domination, flowing being	Openness to ultimate awareness

Crisis?	No	No	Traumatic catharsis	Incomplete	Nearly always	Death and rebirth
Nature of alliance	"Professional" detached	"Professional" friendly	Some transference	Transference	Transference neurosis	Companions in the unknown
Length and commitment	Short-term, minimal investment	Moderate investment, medium term; group methods often especially helpful	Moderate investment, medium term; group methods often especially helpful	Long-term, important life investment	Major life commitment; expectation of true life change even after therapy	Major life commitment; expectation of true life change even after therapy
Life significance	Incidental	Helpful to better life	Important life changes	Life change, enrichment	Basic revision of life perspective	Basic revision of life perspective
Symptoms	Symptom relief	Symptom relief	Symptoms worked through	Symptoms worked through	Symptoms unimportant	Symptoms unimportant
Typical therapy	Behavior modification	Group therapy	General psychotherapy	Ego analysis, depth therapy	Existential psychotherapy	Transpersonal therapy

another. They are constellations of observations, conveniently brought together to aid our discussion. But constellations exist only in the eye of the beholder.

Matching Therapy to Client Needs

With so many levels of therapeutic goals, how do I know how to guide a new client toward the level at which we can best work? I don't. What I do is to start out as though each person were headed for the most thorough-going level—unless, of course, the circumstances of beginning our work together (limited time or funds, clear need to deal with some immediate life situation) make it apparent that it would be inappropriate and contrary to the client's interests to so direct our efforts.

At the beginning with most clients, we work with the intent of moving toward a comprehensive therapeutic goal—emancipation or transcendence. In time I find that some people are not ready to go that far or that with others I do not seem to have the sensitivity or skill to help them make that deep a commitment or undergo that much turmoil. Thus we may work to the growth or even the renewal levels and have a good therapeutic outcome.

The early therapeutic work—establishing a sound working alliance, teaching a broadened conception of one's own nature, developing skills in inner searching, and so on—are solid bases for all the therapeutic levels. (This early work is more demanding and takes client and therapist into more unconscious material than is useful for the first and second—the counseling—levels.) Thus the practical route of building a firm basis for our mutual work will pay off no matter how far we eventually choose to go on this journey. And we both will be better able to assess how far is realistic when we have been working together long enough to have a truly subjective "feel" for what our partnership is like, what the journey we're making is apt to bring about in each of us, and what the costs, of all kinds, are likely to be if we stop short or if we extend it. In this process, hopes are modified by realistic experience, and disappointments have had the corrective of new horizons opening up. The decision that now we jointly, and largely implicitly, arrive at is almost certainly going to be better founded than any we might have made at the outset.

The Focus of This Book

In this book, I am talking about psychotherapy as an enterprise which seeks to reduce anxiety and pain, but which intends going beyond that important function to evoke the potentialities that are latent within each of us. I will not devote much space to the deficiency levels of the scale I've described. There are many excellent presentations of theory and procedure for such work* which the interested reader should consult.

Other Contrasts Among Therapies

Action and Inner Exploration Therapies

Another way of distinguishing and making more understandable the kind of therapy which I'm describing in this book is to contrast it with other approaches. A comparison can be made between therapies that give primary place to action of some kind and those more directed toward subjective exploration. Of course, nearly all therapies are concerned with both, but I am speaking here about relative emphases. This is a contrast that is frequently misunderstood, and I want to try to prevent that confusion now.

Action therapies—for example, Gestalt, bioenergetics, primal, behavior shaping, and some transactional analysis work—may be contrasted with inner exploration therapies, such as psychoanalysis, Jungian analytic therapy, and the present existential-humanistic approach. In action therapies, the focus of attention tends to be on what the therapist does with and to the client. The therapist suggests physical actions, role playing, dialogues with oneself or other important life figures simulated by the client. The inner search therapies, in contrast, place more attention on what the client finds within the client's own stream of awareness when that stream is as little intruded upon (contaminated) as possible by the therapist.

*See for examples Balsam and Balsam (1974); Brammer and Shostrom (1968); Bruch (1974); Burton (1967); Colby (1951); Fromm-Reichman (1950); or Rogers (1951). Nearly all of these books describe therapeutic approaches which go beyond the first two counseling levels as well as dealing with those levels.

Action therapies generally believe that the therapeutic or growth-evoking agency is the *corrective emotional experience* which results from the client discharging old, previously bound-up emotions and freely venting current feelings. The therapist seeks to provide stimuli which will call forth emotions—often seeking almost any emotional release on the hypothesis that once the client begins to experience the catharsis, the important materials will surface spontaneously. In contrast, the inner searching approaches, while valuing the contribution that catharsis can make to releasing dammed up feelings and other subjective material, believe that such working through is most meaningful and constructive when it emerges from the client's own resolving of the resistances and so permitting the release of pent-up feelings and thoughts. The inner-directed approaches certainly recognize the value of the corrective emotional experience also but insist that how that experience comes about is critically important to whether the experience will be corrective (healing or growth fostering). This is a place where the confusion alluded to earlier often occurs. An example may help:

Bill comes for therapy with complaints of being restless and irritable, of losing interest in his work, and feeling out of touch with his family. The action therapist might, after some time spent in developing a good working relation, encourage Bill to beat on a pillow and shout at it angrily—perhaps saying, "No! No! No!" and urge Bill to let go to any emotions which erupt. Hopefully as he did this, Bill would lose the sense of artificiality and would find himself caught up in an old and long repressed rage about, say, his mother's preference for a sibling. Then the action therapist might encourage Bill to talk to an empty chair as though his mother sat in it and to tell his mother of his anger and hurt. Next Bill might be asked to sit in that "mother chair" and reply to Bill. Thus the work would proceed, seeking to help Bill thoroughly ventilate his old hurt, to get new and more mature perspectives on it, and then to feel a release from constrictions he'd long carried and which might well be contributing to his complaints.

A therapist who emphasizes the inner search when working with Bill encourages him to tell his story of his restlessness and poor relationships in his own way. As Bill does so, the therapist is alert to point out ways in which Bill seems inauthentic or avoidant in his account (e.g., "Bill, I notice you seldom mention

> your mother except in a semihumorous way. I wonder if it is hard to talk about your relation with her in straight terms?"). In time Bill would find that he had difficulty or experienced unwanted feelings when trying to describe his relations with his mother authentically. As he confronted this, he might tend to get annoyed with the therapist's repeated comments about his problem in talking genuinely about his relation with his mother ("You really bug me, always making such a big deal out of how I talk about Mom. Why don't you drop it?"). Now the therapist would recognize that some of the irritability of which Bill originally complained was being displayed right in the session and would hypothesize that this was suggestive that this was an area of importance ("Bill, I think you'd rather get into an argument with me than to face up to how much trouble you have really looking at your feelings about your relation with your mother.").
>
> In this fashion and often bringing in other areas of related feelings and difficulty, Bill would be helped to discover the repressed and dreaded feelings and thoughts which operate to upset his life ("You probably think I'm kind of dull compared to your other patients. Well, I don't give a damn. I'm tired of meeting your and everybody else's expectations. I'm just fed up; do you understand? You and my boss and my mother and the whole damn lot of you can just go to hell—and take my wife too! . . .")
>
> Now the catharsis and corrective emotional experience would occur for Bill, but it would likely be in a context of interrelated feelings and ideas which more totally represent Bill's life situation, the way he sees himself, and the possibilities he has for breaking free of the old patterns.

As an inner-search-valuing-psychotherapist, I feel that this latter route leads to more pervasive and lasting results. I believe that when the client comes to his emotional tie-ups as a consequence of his own inner exploration (with the therapist chiefly focusing on the process rather than the content of the patient's work) then more than a corrective emotional experience, valuable as that is, occurs: The client gains in genuine inner vision, in a self-knowing that is more than verbal or logical; it is truly organismic, an experience of the whole being. The client expands inner awareness and in life generally, and that expanded awareness remains a lasting part of the person, enriching subsequent life in many subtle ways.

My examples are both over-simplified, of course. I trust I have not badly distorted the action therapist's approach. It has much to commend it, and I use action methods from time to time in my own work as supplements.

One other contrast is possible with the action therapies: Generally what is regarded as the ideal way for the client to participate in the therapeutic hour is different in the two perspectives. In action therapies, the effort is to have the client intensely emotionally involved as much as possible, in keeping with the emphasis on emotional experience. In inner search work, the ideal client condition is one of being intensely "present"—that is, genuinely and nearly totally in the moment and what is going on. (This concept of "presence" is discussed further in Chapter 3.) The truly present client is totally caught up in delving into subjectivity. This delving—and this is the important point which is often overlooked—is not a matter of "thinking about" or "figuring out" one's self. It is rather an openness to discovery within, which is more similar to meditation or to reading an intensely gripping novel than it is to doing arithmetic problems.

Inner Vision vs. Insight

The concept of presence points to a profound difference between existential-humanistic psychotherapy and the orientation of many psychoanalysts and other insight-valuing therapists. Many of these workers apparently give relatively little attention to the client's presence or expectancies. They concentrate on working out a logical and systematic (often historical) account of the client's dynamics and how they correlate with the theoretical postulates of the therapist's approach to personality. In such therapy, the client often attains extensive knowledge (miscalled *insight*) *about* the self, but little effective inner vision (i.e., a vital sense of one's own intentions and powers in directing one's own life).

Limits to the Existential-humanistic Approach

The kind of therapy this book describes is, to my mind, extremely valuable to many people. It is, in equal truth, quite inappropriate or unsuccessful with others. When there is a fortunate match of client, therapist, and method, immense gains in relief of distress, fostering of growth, and expanding of living can result. That's what this book is about, and I think this is a very humanely important matter. Having said that, let me also say that I cannot (nor can any therapist) help everyone who comes to me. I do not, in fact, believe that any approach works for everyone. Claims to universality rest either on dishonesty or naivete, to my mind. Many systems are helpful, but human beings are too varied, too complex, and too unknown for us to expect that the ultimate psychotherapy will be discovered—or even that it could exist.

2

The Traveler Makes Ready for the Journey: What the Client Brings to Psychotherapy

Having made the decision to go, the traveler must look to the preparations. These preparations certainly include luggage, funds, farewells, and engaging a guide, but more fundamental is the inner getting ready. This requires truly experiencing the fact that a choice has been made and knowing the ambivalence which it brings. It involves letting go of some parts of life which formerly were important. It involves recognizing the subtle differences in feelings about people and places and activities that comes as one knows these things will never be seen in quite the old way again. The most important preparations for the trip—and the ones which may most profoundly affect how the trip will work out—are the subtle and half-conscious alterations within the traveler's own feelings and thoughts.

And so it is that I talk in this chapter about the client coming to the first interview of the psychotherapeutic trip. The client does not arrive with empty expectancy. Much has already transpired that will be deeply important to the work about to be begun. The client comes with a great deal of luggage which is emotional, intellectual, and even spiritual, having to do with the deeper reaches of being.

Two strangers meet by prearrangement; their purpose, to wrestle with life itself; their goal, to win from deadness more life for one of them; their risk, that one or both of them will find life filled with pain and anxiety for some period of time; their certainty that if they persist in good faith with their struggle both will be changed in some measure.

Intensive psychotherapy is pretty much a unique enterprise in our everyday world. The student contemplating becoming a therapist is embarking on a voyage whose outcome can hardly be guessed. Similarly, the client hopes for profound and beneficial changes, but is self-deluded to think to prescribe what they will be.

All of this may seem a bit melodramatic, and I suppose in a way it is. Yet for me and for many of the people with whom I've traveled on the psychotherapy pilgrimage, the journey has indeed brought us to new places in ourselves and with others, to new places we might never have chosen had we the option at the outset; though usually we felt right about them when we finally arrived.

In this and the next chapter, I talk about the two people who make this voyage, the client and the therapist; I talk about them as human beings, not solely as roles or functions. It is important for the reader to sense a kinship with each. Only in this way will there be genuine communication in the rest of the book. For above all else, psychotherapy of the humanistic-existential orientation is a very personal, subjective, and life-changing experience for both participants.

What the Client Brings to the Enterprise

Anxiety and Pain

Look at those two words, "anxiety" . . . "pain." Let them in. Let yourself know what they mean from the inside, not as abstractions, not as something other people experience. If you don't intimately know those words and what they name, you won't understand much of this book. If you can't let them resonate within you, you cannot yet be a truly humanistic therapist; although you may need to be a client in some psychotherapy. If those words speak to you, you are already coming to meet the meanings I want to convey.

The house is quiet. Everyone has gone to sleep. I want to read a little bit yet, to settle down so that sleep will come more readily when I too go to bed. I adjust the cushion in my chair, turn the lamp up a notch, pick up my book, and get settled. It takes two or three tries to make sense of the first sentence; after that it goes well for a page or so. Then I realize I've reread the same sentence three or four times, and I still have no idea what it means.

I didn't want this to happen. I tried to keep busy, to find an interesting book, and to stay up until I would be sleepy enough to fall asleep at once after being convoyed to the edge of sleep by the book. I didn't want this to happen again. But I knew it would.

I can't breathe well. The air seems thin; I need more oxygen. I stir restlessly; the cushion is uncomfortable at my back. My hands feel sweaty. I try to force my eyes back to the book, but they won't focus properly. I squirm in the chair and grab for a big lungful of air. My clothes feel tight and gritty. I can't get my chest to open and receive properly; it's as though I have to tell it how to breathe. My heart feels icy and heavy. Suppose this strain is too much for it? I'm up, out of the chair, walking urgently across the room. Do I want something? I can't think what. No, no, I just need to move. It feels good to move. But I want to run or jump. Walking is too slow, too inactive. I can't walk properly in this small room. Maybe I ought to go outside. The air would be cooler; there'd be more of it. No, that's silly. I can't go out of the house this time of night. Maybe I could open a window and get more air. That won't do any good, I know. I really know I'm just getting upset. I'm anxious. I just need to calm down. Calm down! How can I calm down? I can't even breathe! I'm scared, and I don't know of what. Or I do, but I don't want to know. I'm crazy, what's the matter with me? I'm anxious, anxious.

Anxiety, the fear without a face. Anxiety, the twentieth century's white plague. We have created a world in which we must often live with anxiety. We have split the atom, gone to the moon, solved the riddle of DNA, sped on routine journeys at speeds in excess of the sound of our own travel, developed ever more hideous and efficient weapons, made our central cities human wastelands, torn down the churches, exposed the rotten timbers in our government's edifice, made our schools institutions for holding the children we don't know how to cope with and our prisons schools for crimes from which we can't protect ourselves. Leonard Bernstein titles his composition *The Age of Anxiety*. The time of anxiety is now. How is it that not everyone is knocking on the psychotherapist's door?

Pain

And what is *pain*? Ask yourself, feel into the answer to that question. Pain is so universal a part of the human experience that you may realize with some surprise that it is not easily defined. Pain is hurt; it is an unpleasant and unwelcome subjective sensation, usually linked with injury to the body in our thinking, although by no means solely a bodily experience. Pain is a signal of something amiss, something dangerous or threatening, something requiring attention. Pain is anguish, is torment, is alarm, is the advance courier of death.

Anxiety, the sense of threat and apprehension, may be borne, even though with lowered efficiency and blasted satisfaction in living. But anxiety, when coupled with pain, impels us to action—I can no longer defer seeking help. Usually, but by no means always, the client coming for psychotherapy is experiencing a combination of anxiety and pain.

Pain is a signal that something is wrong in my life system. It may be pain that signals a decayed tooth, a cut finger, an upset stomach, a tumor disrupting the stomach's functioning, or a breakdown in the heart's steady work. It may be a signal of too much guilt, too much conflict and threat with those close to me, a dreaded necessity for decision, emptiness and futility to the daily routine, fear of aging and death, or intolerable loneliness. Pain is the voice of my life crying out for attention, for remedy. (Pain suppressors are life suppressors; tranquilizers are signal denials.)

Desperation

Usually, but not always, the client has gone through a period of trying to live with anxiety and pain and another period of trying to relieve one or both with home remedies—seeking distraction, changing some part of life (residence, job, family, relationships, friends), exerting willpower to suppress the unwanted feelings, and so on. When the client comes to therapy, it is often in desperation, although the fact may be disguised from the therapist and even from oneself. Consciously or not, the client feels pressed toward the panic of being trapped in feelings from which there seems no hope of relief.

The therapist seeing the client for the first time needs to be sensitive to the likely, but often suppressed or hidden, pressures which are motivating that meeting—anxiety, pain, and desperation. High among the therapist's priorities will be making an opportunity for the client to vent these emotions to some extent. Yet, it is often important also to help modulate the pouring out of such feelings, lest the client be terrified by too abrupt a catharsis. It is a powerful experience to have a sympathetic and neutral listener who may have the power to alleviate the load the client has been carrying. Certainly such concerns as the details of the arrangements for therapy, the client's personal history, and similar matters should not be allowed to preempt the opportunity to set down this heavy load, at least briefly and at least in part.

Hope

The entry into psychotherapy comes about not only because the client is plagued with anxiety and pain and is desperate for relief. It also expresses the client's hope that life can be different. This seems so obvious, but we so often overlook it or take it for granted and pay no further attention to it. One's *hope* for oneself is one of the most important things the client brings to the therapeutic work; it will be a resource on which we will draw many times and which must carry the client through literal hell and even, paradoxically, abject hopelessness.

The wise therapist listens fully to the accounts of the client's distress, of the efforts at self-help which did not avail, and of the attempts to make sense of the plight which enmeshes the client.

Then the therapist goes on gently to inquire into the client's hope. Gently indeed, for while a new client may be willing, even eager to tell of trouble, such a person rightly protects hope from unsympathetic eyes and voices. The therapist listens to the hope, not just to see how realistic are the expectations from therapy, although that is important of course and not just to assess readiness for intensive work or for group or for some particular form of therapy although those are certainly significant issues. The sensitive therapist listens as well to learn how this person has clung to the sense of possibility through torment and disappointment, to feel with the client the dim or bright vision of what is latent—i.e., awaiting birth within.

The Client's Self-understanding

Human beings are the creatures who create *meaning.* We must always have meaning or we go mad or die. When we try to find meaning "out there" in the world, in abstractions (life, goodness, "God and country"), or in other people (spouse, children, service to others), or in any other external, then we become the creatures of that external—we lose our autonomy. But we must have meaning. And when we find our anxiety, pain, and desperation pushing us to seek help, we are likely to come to the therapist so that this expert can disclose the meaning that has eluded us. The therapist is often seen, although one seldom puts this into explicit words, as a person who through study and experience has discovered the meaning of being. (And we therapists all too often slip into thinking that this is so also.)

But before the hour of that first interview, the client is already trying to make sense of suffering, of an agonizing plight. One always tries to explain it to oneself and possibly to others, to give it a name at least, to find causes and thereby to suggest possible solutions. How one formulates a way of thinking about distraught emotions, about futile efforts to get relief, about what probably brought the condition on; and about what needs to be done about it—how one puts all of this into some kind of basket of meaning is an important part of what the client brings to that first interview.

Some clients are eager to share their formulations with the therapist; like students who have done their homework, they look for recognition and appreciation for "insight" into themselves. Sometimes clients are reluctant to risk their formulations for fear that the therapist will invalidate them and thus take away the slender comfort they have been given. Sometimes clients want to get the therapist to make formulations as a way of testing whether this expert will be able to see things as they do.

It is important for the therapist to learn how clients formulate their situations, but they must be helped to share this in their own way, rather than having it pulled from them in pieces by therapist questions. Too often, therapists unthinkingly treat clients as though they were inert and had no useful conceptions of their own conditions and needs. Such therapists are apt to go through a schedule of questions to which they want responses provided directly and without elaboration. Or, if they encourage elaboration, such therapists may be listening only to detect symptoms and observe thought processes, but without any recognition of the deeper meaning of what these human beings are expressing about their unique encounters with life.

How clients formulate their situation before they come to therapy is a tremendously important matter. It will tell the humane and aware therapist how each person grapples with life, what sorts of meanings are most helpful, what roles various resources (family, friends, reading, popular media) play in helping to give sense to experiences, how these people deal with their own internal living (pain, anxiety, fears, hopes, wants), and much more. And over and beyond these, the clients' views of their own plights will often have much that is accurately pointing to the directions in which the therapy must work—even though those accounts are seldom sufficient.

Coming for Help

When the day finally comes on which the client will meet the therapist and begin the psychotherapeutic journey, a process long in maturing is being completed. The roots of the trip into that office for the first time extend back, almost certainly, to the person's earliest days. One of the first learnings the human being makes is how safe it is to be helpless, and coming for psychotherapy reveals one's helplessness, or so it seems to a great many people on the first day. It is so familiar as to be hackneyed that the client will see the therapist as father or mother (or both), as teacher, or other authority figure. And this begins well before the first visit. As one contemplates consulting a therapist, one can only do so by creating in imagination a therapist. And what are the materials from which this figure is made? From those I have just listed, of course, but also from a favorite aunt or uncle, from a minister or priest, from the cartoons of patients lying on couches saying ridiculous things, from novels and movies about therapy, from one's own deep hope for someone who can truly understand and really help.

In the same way, the client prepares before that first contact. Thought is given to the formulation of one's plight, of course, but one thinks also of secrets fearful to reveal, of the aspects of oneself in which one takes pride and which one hopes will stand the test of professional scrutiny, and of the little hopes and fears that dart through awareness unexpectedly, which one cherishes yet feels childish about. A person thinks, too, of what is known about therapy or what has been heard and wondered about as to whether it is so: Will the therapist insist on five times a week? Will the client get attached to and dependent on that unknown and strange other? Will therapy force one to face conflicts with a spouse or parent that have long been kept walled off? Will there be the risk of divorce or rupture with parents, of losing or quitting a job—all of which are rumored to frequently happen. Will one at last get a chance to let out that secret part, that poet or dreamer, that lost creative self? Will the therapist be silent and unresponsive? Will it all take a long time and a lot of money? Can a person really be so selfish as to expend so much on one's own needs? Why can't one just get hold of oneself and handle one's own problems? Is it a sign of being weak or defective in some way to have to have help of this kind?

Encounter and Engagement

And so the two strangers meet. They look at each other, listen to each other, sniff the air between them. Their invisible antennae gently stretch out, tentatively probing and gingerly assessing. Their intuitions, working consciously and far below consciousness, take stock. One silently thinks, "Is this someone I can believe in? Someone I can trust with my secrets, my guilts, and shames, my tender and deep hopes for my life, my vulnerability?" The other wonders,

"Is this someone I can invest in? Someone I can stand by in pain and crisis? Someone I can make myself vulnerable to? What surprise may this person bring forth, and what may that surprise trigger within me?"

In a thousand subtle and implicit ways this measuring and estimating goes on. It is a critically important process, and only some portion of it can be made conscious, verbal, or open. It is much too important a process to be transacted by any agencies, but the actual and total persons most to be involved. (I am aware that many settings call for the client to be seen by an intake worker who makes the assignment to the therapist. This may be administratively efficient, but I believe very strongly that the assignment should only be a recommendation, subject to the outcome of the first encounter of client and therapist and thus to their deeper reading of how they come together.)

Now both must make decisions. Shall we go ahead? Shall we use a period of a few weeks or a month to test how we feel together, or shall we make a longer commitment now? This is a serious business, and it needs to be done with sobriety and the recognition that once committed these two people may become wedded in a way that will be more intimate, at least in some dimensions, than any other relationship in the client's life, and certainly powerfully involving for the therapist as well. There are practically no equivalent occasions in life when such a major choice will be made without the tide of emotion carrying one, as in a decision to marry.

But the decision to work together does not ensure a genuine engagement in the sense I am using the word here; that kind of bond must be forged from actual experience of each other. It begins with the first tentative touchings at the emotional level—the client lets go of pent-up emotions or reveals a long withheld secret. The therapist stands steady, shows empathy but is not swept away, seems to see beyond the immediate to the person who is potential in the client. The bond begins to form. There are times of misunderstanding or perhaps even of conflict. The client is anxious to please and yet resentful of the need to please. Risking so much, the client watches to see whether the therapist is solidly present, open to being affected, but able to withstand being captured. The therapist begins to find points of personal identification and difference with the client and between this particular client and others. Each is emerging as a distinct individual to the other, and they begin to be genuinely engaged at a deep working level.

A Client's Own Account of Beginning Psychotherapy

I asked several former clients to describe some of their experiences in psychotherapy, and I'll use excerpts from those accounts at various points. Names and identifying material have been changed, and some shortening of the accounts has occurred; otherwise the descriptions are unaltered. The following is from a professional man's recollection of his first interview:

> Here it is, Baby—the moment you've been avoiding your whole damn life! The verbal agility, the intelligence, the finely honed wit, the Princeton degree, the fancy threads, all the psychology books I've read the past six months—what good is it all now? Well, maybe a little—he might be a little impressed. Please? Not for long, though. He's trained to see through this kind of jazz. For once in my life I gotta face the fact that all this window-dressing is going to get me exactly nowhere. . . This man is here to see through all this shit . . . to the shit below it. I am paying him to peel it away, layer by layer, like a giant onion, painfully, slowly, piece by piece, until he finally gets down to . . . what? Hey—that's funny! What am I afraid of? There's nothing down there below all that. I'm an act through and through. Nothing at all. Nothing? Why does that word hang there like that?
>
> That last year in college was the only time I can really say I enjoyed myself. It hasn't been the same since. This graduate school trip just isn't doing it for me. It's boring; it's mechanical; it's too much pressure; it's . . ." Graduate school—yeah! . . . How'm I doing? He doesn't show it, but you can bet he's getting the right picture. Princeton graduate, precocious artistic genius—did I tell him about the summer I had a real gallery show? Art versus science. A conflict between two worthy goals. That's it. Play that one up. That one should carry me at least three sessions. Renaissance Man, Da Vinci in modern dress. Torn between two worlds, art and science. Okay, I'm set till the end of the hour. Safe. No way he can possibly . . .

"Don, tell me—what are you experiencing as you tell me about these things?"

Thud. Silence. Why can't I say anything? Why is the room dark all of a sudden? Come on—this is absurd. This guy is a human being, just like me, with glasses, tie, and beard, just like me, and he just asked me a simple routine question. Big deal. Then . . . why is it I can't put three words together to make an answer? Let's go, let's get back in gear. He said experiencing? What the hell does he mean by that? He must mean what am I thinking. I'm *telling* him what I'm thinking! What more does he want? I'm telling him why I'm here, what's bothering me; I'm telling him all about myself. And it's a damn good story, if I do say so myself. Isn't he listening? Wait a minute—I haven't told him about Grace yet. I was saving that for next time. He wants problems—that's it—not history. I better skip to that right now . . .

"Don, listen—will you try something for me? Let's stop conversing for a minute, so you can get in touch with what's going on inside you right now. Take your time. Then come on back and see if you can't tell me a little about what you find. Okay?"

Holy shit! That's what I thought he meant! . . . Jesus H. Christ—how am I gonna get out of this one? What's going on inside?! What's going on inside is . . . oh my—God! He can't mean *this* shit! Nah . . . please. You can't mean that. Well fuck you! Nobody hears this stuff, but nobody! Even you! Besides, it's trivial, irrelevant. I'm here with some Big Problems. Career indecision. Unfulfilled potential. Existential angst. Trouble getting laid. I'm not here to spray out all this noise in my head . . . I am not going to waste my time on the kind of garbage I'm thinking right now. Why doesn't he say anything? Trying to wait me out, eh? Go ahead—try me . . . I suppose I could tell him to go to Hell. Uh uh. Too crude. Doesn't fit my image. I could split and not come back. Great! Then I'm right back where I started and, believe me, that is no victory . . .

Five years it takes you to get up the nerve to do this, you walk in and he says "tell me what you're experiencing" and you're ready to pack up and go back to your zilch of a life and probably end up suiciding rather than let the truth out. The truth. That you're really a pathetic creep. A terrified, shy, lonely, weak, ugly, disgusting asshole. A poor excuse for a human being. With a Princeton degree to throw people off the scent. Something only a mother could love—and even she didn't quite carry it off. God, what a hoax you are! Everything you've ever done, everything you've ever said, everything to be a Big Shot so people wouldn't know. So they wouldn't know what I'm really like. Well at least that's something. Things may be bad, but can you imagine what would be coming down if they really knew? . . . Can't you see? It isn't worth it. I *can't* tell you what's going on in here. I may be alone, but at least people talk to me . . . See, Doctor, that's what you fail to appreciate. There's risk involved here, and I'm not kidding. I'm not saying this just to you, but to everyone I've ever faced—if you only knew me, I mean what I'm really like, if you really got to step into my head and listen to this garbage, the ball game would be all over. For good. I don't have much in this life but, believe me, if any of this shit ever came out, I'd lose even that. Can you guarantee me it's worth that risk? Can you even guarantee that *you* wouldn't run away screaming? No, I guess you can't. No guarantees . . . God, it'd be a relief to dump some of this shit for once in my life. I been carrying it around so goddamn long.

Just him, nobody else, right? Can I trust him? I wonder if he sits around with his cronies at night and trades stories about weirdos like me. Nah, somehow he doesn't look the type . . . What do I really have to lose? Could things possibly get worse? The thing is, I think they could. They could get a lot worse. He could confirm my worst suspicions about myself, for starters. He could give up right at the beginning, refer me to some crony who treats the *real* freaks . . . You haven't met one like me before. And goddamit, it matters to me what you think. I mean what you'll think when I really level with you. The others never know me. But you will. Jesus, I hope you'll like me! That you'll want to be my friend. That you'll find something in me that's worth something to you. Can I even hope?

"I have the sense, Don, that there's a lot going on in you right now. Could you share some of it?"

Persistent bastard, isn't he? Okay, Doctor B. You win. God help me if you don't know what you're doing, if this bombs out. Jesus Christ, I guess this is it. Here goes . . .

3

The Guide Makes Preparations as Well: Some Specifications for an Ideal Therapist

Even as the traveler is getting ready, the guide is doing so also. Such preparations draw on the guide's whole career, on experiences, learning, skills, and whatever wisdom has been attained. The veteran guide knows that the journey ahead will be hazardous for the traveler and that it may have hidden dangers for the guide as well. Hard-won wisdom says that the person who goes on the journey can never be the one who returns from it. At least some subtle sea changes always are worked on those who travel. This traveler—as each unique client does—will take the guide into unfamiliar territory in which the guide's lore will be helpful but never enough, in which the success or failure of the venture will ultimately be determined by the traveler and not the guide. So the guide seeks to be as ready as possible, knowing it is never possible to be as ready as desirable.

Now we look to the qualities that go to make up an ideal therapist to accompany the client's inner explorations. I will describe what I think is involved in being such a therapist. I will emphasize personal qualities more than technical knowledge. This, be it noted, is not because knowledge is unimportant but because it should be so thoroughly incorporated as to be implicit in the therapist's whole way of being (Bugental, 1965, Chapter 26).

Desirable Qualities in the Therapist

Who is the Therapist?

What a strange thing to be a psychotherapist! I who always wondered how to do things rightly, how to be like other people, how to succeed and be valued! How strange that today I am seen by others as someone who can help them do those things that I tried for so long to do and felt so continually I could not do! I guess in a way I was always in training to be a therapist, though I was well into adult life before I even heard of that vocation. I can't remember now, but I suppose I must have known about psychiatrists and psychoanalysts; although I'm sure that, to whatever extent I ever thought of them, they seemed as distant as the pyramids, and I had as little thought I'd ever see one, let alone be one.

It's said that most of us who become therapists do so to solve our own problems. I didn't follow that path consciously, but I think it probably exerted an unconscious pull. After I'd already chosen to be a psychologist, there was the sense of personal relevance and the hope of finding resolutions for some of my own struggles. (I've described some of this seeking and those struggles in Bugental, 1976, Chapter 8.)

The Therapist's Own Well-being

How can someone who's messed up himself help someone else get unmessed up? That's a question with a lot of meanings in it.

First of all, being messed up is not a sure sign of being in a bad place in life. In fact, as I pointed out in the first chapter, being adjusted in today's world may be being more messed up. That's not the same thing as saying that being messed up is a good thing or even an all right thing. Being messed up—being anxious, conflicted, self-doubting—is no fun; that's for sure. Moreover it's wasteful of life, of human potential, and of what might be renewing and more fulfilling for a person.

The bottom line, it seems to me, is this: The ideal psychotherapist is one who seeks to get and keep his or her act together. The ideal therapist recognizes that the emotions, conflicts, biases, and anxieties of the therapist's own life inevitably have their effects on the client's life, and this is not an idle recognition. Thus the ideal therapist accepts the responsibility for continuing self-monitoring to reduce the untoward impact of the therapist's distresses on the client. To this end, the therapist seeks personal therapy not only in the early or training stages, but at any point in life at which those distresses intrude into the therapeutic work. Moreover the ideal therapist makes use of other means to reduce such intrusions —meditation, tuning in to dreams, or consultation with peers or with colleagues of greater experience. In short, though the therapist can never be expected to be "clear," without emotional or other hang-ups, the therapist most certainly can be expected to be one who makes more than usual efforts to be aware of and do something about those hang-ups.

So, if psychotherapists don't necessarily bring their own having it all together to the meeting with their clients, what do they bring? Well, the answer is pretty obvious: there's no standard brand psychotherapist, and there is no guaranteed content of the package that has that name. Accordingly, I'll describe some attributes that seem to me to be pretty important for the therapist to have or to be working at developing. No therapist I know—and that surely includes me—has all of these to the ideal point; many therapists I respect are concerned about trying to grow on these dimensions and are doing a damn good job of it too.

Commitment: Being a "Pro"

The ideal therapist is a "pro." By that term I am talking about an attitude, not making a contrast with being an amateur in terms of whether the therapist gets paid for doing therapy. I've known therapists who were truly pros, but who contributed their services in a nonprofit clinic; what I'm talking about is much more an inner process in the person. To my way of thinking there are four distinguishing characteristics of the true pro in whatever field that person works.

The Pro Draws a Sense of Personal Identity from the Work. Without conscious deliberation I make choices, respond to what I encounter differently, and react to issues in terms of my affiliation with the field of psychotherapy. I am not just someone who "does psychotherapy"; I am a psychotherapist.

The Pro, Knowing That One Can Always Improve Professionally, Has a Dedication to Doing So. The pro is self-motivated to grow and sets personal standards for achievement. The pro does not continue to develop because an employer or state agency says this is required but because of a sense of personal emergence.

The Pro Has a Considered Perspective on the Field of Work and the Relationships with Those Worked With. The pro takes time to think about the meaning of the work, about the values involved, about the way the work fits into the broader society, and about the effects of the work on other people.

The Pro Realizes That One's Own Being Is the Primary Avenue Through Which One Can Realize One's Vocational Potential. It is not the knowledge which one has but how it is integrated, interpreted, and applied which distinguishes the true pro.

Dedication to the Healing/Growth Process

One of the most fundamental characteristics of the ideal therapist is a conviction, born of experience as well as of theory, that the intrinsic healing/growth process of the client can be trusted. What this means is that such a therapist knows full well that no one can heal or cure or even directly "therap" the client. At a gut level, one learns that the only force which can produce genuine and lasting change is the power and thrust of the client toward greater realization of what is potential within. The therapist who knows this deeply does not waste her or his own or the client's time and emotions trying to do what cannot be done: solve the client's problems, guide the client's life choices, or urge forth the client's latent capacity for living more fully. Instead such a therapist concentrates on aiding the client in recognizing and releasing the blocks that keep the *aliveness* uneasily imprisoned within.

We will talk a number of times and in various ways about this power that each of us has to revitalize our own living, to deal with the concerns of our lives, and to free ourselves from *thingness*. For now, I want only to begin to sketch in some of the ways in which this capacity is expressed and the corresponding points to which the therapist may most usefully direct attention.

Presence: An Essential for Psychotherapy

Existentialists—philosophers, psychotherapists—make much of the quality of "being there" (*dasein*). We, in more everyday thinking, recognize the same characteristic as important when we talk about someone who isn't "all there" or say that we're having trouble "getting with it" when a speaker is dull. I think one of the most important essentials to tapping into the healing/growth process is to call on the client to be truly present in the work of the therapy hour. Now that may seem a matter of course, but let me assure you it is anything but. I'll offer a formal definition of presence first, and then I'll try to illustrate how elusive it can be and how important it is to work for it.

> *Presence* is the quality of being in a situation in which one intends to be as aware and as participative as one is able to be at that time and in those circumstances. Presence is carried into effect through mobilization of one's inner (toward subjective experiencing) and outer (toward the situation and any other person/s in it) sensitivities.

Presence is immensely more than just being there physically, it is obvious. It's being totally in the situation. When my client, Ben, comes to talk with me about his life and his anxiety and distress, but begins the hour with socializing which seems likely to go on indefinitely, he's not being present. When Lois tells me about the break-up of her marriage in a sarcastic and distant way as though she were relating a story for my amusement, I can feel that she isn't truly present. Presence is being there in body, in emotions, in relating, in thoughts, in every way.

Does it really matter? Yes, it matters very much, and it matters in two fundamental ways. First, what a person does when avoiding presence is to resist the very task for which that person came to therapy, thus enacting the patterns which keep the client from truly having life. Second, what goes on in the therapy hour when either or both my client and I are not truly present will be of less effect in evoking the client's healing/growth powers. I will return to the first of these points in the chapter on the main work of the therapeutic process itself. Now I want to elaborate on the second, since it is the therapist's conviction about the fundamental place of this healing/growth process which is the focus of our attention at the moment. In order to do so, I want to introduce several more concepts.

Although fundamentally presence is a unitary process or characteristic of a person in a situation, accessibility and expressiveness may be identified as its two chief aspects.

> *Accessibility* comes about from one's having the intention to allow what happens in a situation to matter, to have an affect on one. It involves a reduction of the usual social defenses against being influenced or affected by others. It implies a measure of trust and vulnerability.
>
> *Expressiveness* arises from the intent to let oneself be known by the other in a situation, to make available some of the contents of one's subjective awareness without distortion or disguise. It implies a measure of commitment and a willingness to put forth some effort.

Presence, accessibility, and expressiveness are all continua—that is, they are all matters of degree. They vary in terms of the particular person, the situation, the other person(s) present, and many other influences.

Thus one can think of two sides of the matter of presence: the intake side and the output side. Is my client going to be so solidly here that what happens in our time together will have a chance to make a difference, to get through genuinely?

> Betty has had three husbands—one after the other—by the time she is thirty, and she is smart enough to know that an

important part of the reason must be something in herself. So she comes to therapy, and for the first four months she tells her story with tears and pain and fright that are very real. Then comes a new period in which she has difficulty in finding anything important to say, in which she is distractible and irritable. And in which she turns on the charm for my benefit. She wears blouses that gape open or are very nearly transparent; her slacks are so tight they are like a thin skin over her lower body, and she looks at me longingly and invitingly as she talks superficially about her current boy friend, about trying to find a dependable hair dresser, and about other matters equally pointless. Betty isn't here, isn't present, isn't about to be accessible, except in an old, familiar, and self-defeating way.

Handling threat

What happens so the client takes flight in this way? How can someone who has a measure of insight into the source of searing pain and real fright goof off so obviously—and at a fairly stiff fee per hour? Very readily; in fact, it's almost inevitable, even essential, that it will happen. Betty exhausted the familiar territory of her unhappiness; to go ahead she had to open up new and unexplored areas—obviously the only place her *unconscious* contribution to her unhappiness could be—and she was frightened to do so. So Betty-who-was-hurting-and-scared got replaced by Betty-who-knows-how-to-handle-men-and-uncomfortable-situations. Betty's not stupid, but Betty is fearful of what she may discover in the hidden places within herself. Don't make any mistake about it, so are we all. That's why we keep those things locked up.

Now think about what happened here with Betty, for a lot of the picture of intensive therapy is wrapped up right in this little vignette. The client comes in distress; the distress is familiar and can be related without increased discomfort and often with a good feeling of relief—bringing out the pain usually feels good, and besides here's the doctor who's going to make it better. But then the story's told; now what? The doctor isn't doing any miracles; there's not much else to say, or at least not much that feels good to say. So the client draws on a repertoire of ways of meeting uncomfortable situations. These may include being demanding ("I've told you what's bothering me; now you've got to do something to help me"), being pitiful ("It hurts so much; surely you can do something; I've tried everything and nothing helps"), being stoic or indifferent ("I know everybody has it rough and I'm not bellyaching about it, but . . ."), or perhaps being seductive to get someone else to move in and head off the need to go into the dark and frightening places— This is Betty's gambit.

All of the ways I've suggested, and the many, many others that we humans are capable of, can be boiled down to not being accessible to the clear message of the therapy situation: "Hang in and explore within yourself what is really important to you." (They are also in a way failures of expressiveness too, but that's secondary since the patient is not consciously withholding material in the situations I'm describing, but is simply avoiding "knowing" what the real situation is (i.e., the necessity to continue exploring within).

But there is another and very important significance to what's going on at this point. The client, in using a uniquely familiar way of resisting an anxiety-evoking situation, is bringing right into the therapy room (and the relationship) one of the main processes which contributes to not having life as the client wants it to be, to a feeling of impotency in self-direction. Betty's falling back on her sexual appeal, and her abandonment of her own centered seeking within herself is doubtlessly one of the important patterns contributing to her getting into foredoomed relations with men. She isn't so much looking for an adult life companion as for a lifesaver to save her from frightening situations.

To Intervene or Not to Intervene

So do we just tell her about it? "Hey, Betty, guess what? You're doing it right now with me. You're playing sex kitten instead of being a grown-up lady running your own life. So stop it, and go be more mature and everything will work out." No way! She doesn't really know what she's doing, and telling her in some direct way (even not so ham-handedly as in my illustration) just won't work. Moreover the reason grown-up Betty has to resort to this poor strategem must lie in some way she feels about herself (perhaps that she feels women are basically weak or that she sees herself as in some way not really a mature person), and until that underlying basis for her failure to trust herself is dealt with she has to have some device for getting around, so to speak. So for these and other very good reasons we go slowly and concentrate on her lack of presence, helping her to become more accessible. In this way, we prepare the way for helping Betty make a truly fundamental change. Later chapters will describe this whole process more fully.

When the client is having trouble with expressiveness, it is often evidenced by being silent for some time, by evasiveness, by using polite and formal ways of talking, by suppressing or minimizing emotions, or by remaining narrowly factual or objective in what is said. Again these ways of "resisting" being fully present are in themselves important to the therapeutic work (Bugental, 1965, Chapter 6). They display the patterns through which the client has in the past sought protection from what seemed overwhelming threat, ways that now are being continued inappropriately in the therapeutic situation and, more importantly, in the client's life generally. Thus they have important bearings on the very distresses which bring the client to therapy, but they are usually not conscious at the outset. Bringing them to awareness is the work of therapy.

"Real life" significance

I've already said it implicitly, but the point is so important I want to make it quite explicit. Psychotherapy of this kind, which focuses on resolving the resistances to being authentically present in one's life, is not a treatment in an artificial situation (as some writers and therapists see therapy) that must then generalize to the "real life" of the client. Existential-humanistic psychotherapy such as I am describing works with the actual life patterns of the client as they are laid bare in the very real therapeutic confrontation. When such therapy does its work well, the results are changes in the client's very way of structuring life, and thus there is no further step of generalization required.

When I say that in my view the ideal therapist has a firm dedication to the healing/growth process, I mean that such a therapist knows that work is to be done with the naked stuff of the client's life and that only the client can and should make changes in that fragile-durable, elusive-omnipresent, hidden-exposed living matter.

Such a therapist knows, respects, and gladly serves this fundamental truth, and knows too that the therapist's own presence is the key element which must be brought to that work.

Cultivated Sensitivity

Sensitivity is a word that has gotten into trouble. For some people *sensitivity training* is a name for a kind of brainwashing; for others it signifies a kind of encounter group experience which seems out of date now. In other contexts, *sensitive* is used to mean overly tender or sentimental. ("He's too sensitive"; "Don't talk about that in front of her; she's sensitive on the subject.") Despite these bad associations, I want to redeem the word for our use here because better than any other it says precisely what I want to say.

The ideal therapist has refined (polished, developed, trained) sensitivity (the use of all senses, including intuition). That sensing is like a fine instrument, capable of picking up clues that the average person might not register: nuances of meaning, intonations of voice, subtle changes of facial expression or body posture, hesitations, slips of speech, and all the thousand and one subtle expressions of a person in the midst of life. To such an observer, human beings are more like flames than machines; they continually flicker and shift, and the attentive sensing will be aware during a single therapy hour of literally thousands of large and small changes, each expressive of the ongoing inner life. Of course, the therapist doesn't consciously note and record all of this. Cultivated sensitivity makes it possible to sort out what is most significant and to detect the patterns without disrupting attention to all else that is going on. Symphony conductors lead more than a hundred musicians playing at once, and can detect the measure at which a particular violinist came in slightly behind tempo. In many artistic and highly skilled fields refined sensitivity is the essential ingredient of superior competence. So it is with psychotherapy.

Patterns of sensitivity

I am convinced that all of us are born with a far greater capacity for sensitivity to human experience than we manifest in our later years. So much of the training of childhood is a shaping of the areas in which we will keep and refine our empathic sensing and those in which we will blunt it or deny it altogether. In such a way we come to a very partial experience of our own natures and of the world we inhabit. We learn to pick up early and minimal hints to the feelings and attitudes of those who can be the source of rewards and punishments—parents, older brothers and sisters, teachers, the toughest kid in the neighborhood. We develop callouses over our feelings for pain or distress which may involve us beyond our felt limits. Intuition is called into question, and candid reading of those with whom we deal is discovered to be handicapping, impolite, or even hazardous. Everyone knows stories of small children saying out loud what everyone might have sensed but avoided acknowledging ("Why is that man so sad?" "He doesn't like you, does he?")

Sensitivity grows and becomes more subtle and dependable as it is regularly used, trusted, and corrected by careful follow-up. Conscious and unconscious constrictions of sensitivity both tend to distort its acuity and to confuse our communications and relations with others. Effective psychotherapists are those who accept the need continually to cultivate their intuition, empathy, and sensing of human experience, who are alert to discover and remedy blind spots, and who know the areas in which they are apt to send distorted and biasing messages to their clients.

Each therapist has a unique pattern of areas of open receptivity, areas of partial interference in which it is harder for the client's experiences to get through, and areas of relative or absolute blindness. I have learned something of my own patterns: I am alert to clues to sadness, conflict, and sensuality. I pick up without effort Joel's warm feelings toward me, Lois's feelings of bodily restlessness, Pete's anxiety around endings and death, and Nell's reluctance to deal with her deeper yearnings for a creative outlet for life. But when Nell begins to feel her rage at her husband, when Pete feels irritable and rebellious with me, when Lois needs to talk about the fear of aging, or Joel is determined to ferret out an elusive early childhood memory, then I am apt to need clearer signals to bring me to sensitive receptivity.

Of course, I can't say with any surety what my own blind spots are, for if I'm aware of them, they are no longer blind spots. I'm pretty sure they exist, however, and I value feedback from friends, patients, and colleagues—even as I resist it—which can help me become more aware. In addition, with certain clients I will have particular patterns of positive and negative responses. As best I can, I try to keep aware of these, working out those that are chiefly from my own needs, while giving rein to those that seem to foster greater client inward searching.

One obstacle to therapist sensitivity that is apt to be hard for its bearer to recognize is devotion to some theory of therapy. I try to keep alert to this tendency in myself, but again and again I am chagrined to discover that I am hearing the client with my anti-behavioristic, anti-psychoanalytic, pro-existential, pro-humanistic filtering system firmly in place. Periodically I set myself to attend solely to the concrete and immediate presentation of the client, trying to hear it cleanly. Of course, this is never completely possible. We always hear our conversational partners, in or out of therapy, with some expectancies operating. Yet it is possible and desirable to keep aware of those pre-sets and to loosen their constrictions deliberately from time to time.

Other obstacles to true sensitivity are the tendency to listen too much to the *content* of what the client says and to miss the *way* in which it is said. The how of the client's talking—the "process" dimension in contrast to the content—is a rich source of information and a crucial avenue to dealing with the client's presence or lack of it. My examples earlier of clients who were not truly present in their talk are illustrations of what might be missed if one listened solely to the content of what each of those people was saying.

Skills

As sensitivity has to do with the therapist's accessibility, so skills relate to the pro's expressiveness. The two together underscore the importance of the therapist being genuinely present to meet the client's presence in the engagement of the therapeutic hour.

Years ago I heard the story of the client who came to his hour with his tape recorder in hand. "Doc," he said, "I had such a powerful dream last night that the first thing this morning I recorded everything I could remember about it and everything I could associate to it. It's so important that you've got to hear this before we can do anything else. So I'll just start it playing here and then go down to the coffee shop and have the breakfast I didn't have time to get before coming here." With that he started his recorder and left. A few minutes later the therapist slipped onto the stool next to the client in the coffee shop. The latter looked surprised, and the therapist said, "Well, I missed my breakfast too; so I just set up my tape recorder to take down your dream and associations. I'll listen to them later on."

The story creates the image of the two tape recorders solemnly carrying on the work of therapy while the two people visit over their coffee and donuts. But the story illustrates a common misconception of many people including some therapists. The content of what is said—the dream and its associations—are thought to exist independently of the client and the therapist or of their being together or even of the particular day and hour of their meeting.

If any real therapeutic work was accomplished that day, it was in the coffee shop, not the consulting room.

Therapist skills are subtle matters to specify since in such a fundamental way they are the communication skills we all share—with a difference. The difference is the particular form of cultivation given to develop sensitivity and effectiveness in responsiveness, in putting forth ideas, in summoning feelings, in empathic sharing, in effective confronting, and in appropriate supporting.

The fact that the therapist's skills are those of everyday life brings some people to the well-intentioned but quite erroneous conclusion that psychotherapy itself is only, or is best, when it is untrained, undisciplined, and completely spontaneous. Nothing could be further from the truth. Instead, I believe the therapist who is a true "pro" and who is fully responsible in this calling is continually engaged in refining therapeutic knowledge and skill. Just as an accomplished pianist (or any artist) is one who has thoroughly mastered the fundamentals of the craft in order to be free to be truly creative in expression, so the master therapist has incorporated the mechanics of the processes to the point that they are invisible. The pianist no longer "plays the piano" but only draws music forth from the instrument which has become integral to the artist. The therapist no longer "does therapy" but relates so authentically with the client because the skills are integrated completely into the professional's way of being.

A Personal Epilogue

For me, being a therapist has been an immensely enlivening, broadening, and instructive experience. It has also been at times frightening, the source of anguish and personal confrontation. Still and all, I feel like one of the lucky ones, one of those who looks at the day's activity with relish. Now, in my later years, I am enjoying a further yield in discovering a pleasure in reflecting on what I have observed and then teaching and writing about it, as I am doing in this book which we are sharing.

4

The Guide Must Know and the Traveler Must Trust the Vessel: The Fundamental Healing/Growth Process

The choosing of the vessel on which the journey will be made must be largely the responsibility of the guide, who must know the various ships, their special characteristics, their dependability, their speed, and their hazards. The traveler's life will soon be risked aboard the vessel thus selected. Some travelers will have their own views as well, but ultimately most will have to trust the guide's greater experience of such voyages.

The client chooses a therapist in part on the basis of what is believed to be the therapist's views about human beings and about the therapeutic process. Often the client comes with rather fixed ideas—"I don't want any of that groupie stuff," "I had one of those analytic types who never say anything, and I don't want any more of that," "None of that childhood stuff." Sometimes these prescriptions are born as much of the client's unwitting fear as of knowledge, but in any case the therapist does well to give them sober attention and honest answers.

The Fundamental Importance of Concern

A person comes to psychotherapy out of a *sense of possibility,* a feeling that there is the potential for life to be different than it has been. This difference may—for a given person at a particular time—be a hope that there will be less pain or anxiety, a seeking for greater realization of inner possibilities, a quest for improved relations with others, or a belief that there are richer possibilities for life than one has known thus far. Sometimes the sense of possibility is most consciously in the form of looking for a solution to a life problem situation—e.g., pervasive and continual feelings of loneliness or guilt or fear; feelings that one is repeatedly bringing unhappiness on oneself or that one is caught in a circumstance (marriage, vocation, relationship) which is painful and frustrating but which can't be improved or discarded. In brief, a person comes to intensive psychotherapy intending life to be different and willing to explore the possibility that change in one's self will make that difference actual.

I find it useful to have a name for this constellation of feelings which include the following:

the experience of distress, pain, or anxiety (not always consciously);
the yearning for new possibilities in life;
the readiness to make some commitment to self-exploration; and
the hope that change within oneself may be the way to realize the desired possibility.

The word *concern* or *life concern* will be used in this way. In the following pages I will sketch a basic perspective for thinking about the enterprise of intensive psychotherapy. The concept of concern as I've just defined it is pivotal to this view.

The Capacity for Dealing with a Life Concern

Ultimately the capacity to deal with a life concern exists chiefly within the person having that concern. The word "deal" in that postulate needs to be clarified. I don't mean that there aren't very real problems caused by circumstances in the world in which we live. That would be naive. And I certainly don't mean that a person ought to just take those circumstances for granted and not try to change them. In fact, I'm convinced that the healthier we are the less readily we sit still for some of the insanities that are taken for granted in our world. But I do mean that recognizing what we're doing to go along with the pressures from the outside, assessing where and how we can try to bring about changes in those pressures, and mobilizing our most effective efforts to do just that—all of these are most apt to be successfully carried through if we are straight within ourselves. The basis for dealing with a life concern is in the person having that concern even if the way to deal with it is to go out and change things in job, marriage, friendships, or some other way.

Of course, there are a lot of concerns in which the most important sources of difficulty are right here at home in our own ways of being. The way we relate to others, the extent to which we take on needless blame or embarrassment, the difficulties we have in getting our act together and using our powers for our own best interests, the confusions we get lost in between our *wants* and our *shoulds* —all these and many other concerns are not to be solved by changing spouses, work, schools, or anything else—though eventually any of those may be helpful. The main work is to be done right inside of our own heads, guts, and perspectives.

There is something that comes close to being a "general law" of human life that operates here. (We don't have many such almost-always-es in psychology, particularly humanistic psychology, so this is worth noting.) It is this:

> The person having a genuine life concern—experiencing a true sense of dissatisfaction with his or her way of living and a feeling of possibility for it to be different—*will* act in some fashion to reduce that concern.

What this means is that when I'm truly anxious or pained about some aspect of my life or genuinely hopeful for some new possibility, I will do something about that feeling. I won't just forget it or decide it's not important or even just live with the concern. Genuine concern leads to action of some kind. This doesn't mean, of course, that we solve all of our problems, get all our wishes fulfilled, or realize all of our potentials. It's no news to anyone beyond the age of five that there's no "happy ever after."

This general principle does mean that when I have a genuine life concern, I will change my way of looking at things, get into a different life situation, cause the important people in my life to do things differently, learn some new skills, drop some old habits, or in some other way deal with that concern. It doesn't mean that I'll necessarily do something desirable, successful, healthful, or even satisfying about that concern. I may become more mature in relation to it, but I might also regress to a kind of catatonic immobility. I may seek more satisfaction in life through working for social and political change, or I might take a car full of guns and go out shooting people. I may find deeper resources in myself through a spiritual discipline, or I might become obsessed with trying to keep my environment totally germ free and antiseptic. I may try to make my family relationships more deeply rewarding, or I might become a petty tyrant at home, brandishing temper tantrums or hypochondriacal complaints.

The point does not need elaboration. The generalization is simply that one who has a genuine life concern (not a trivial or passing irritation) does something about it in some way—enriching life or constricting it, becoming more healthy or generating symptoms. Psychotherapy can be a means toward guiding the operation of that principle in what will hopefully be desirable and satisfying ways.

Blocks to the Use of Life-changing Capacity

A person comes to psychotherapy because of impaired ability to use latent resources in dealing with the life-changing concern. Were we not in some way handicapping ourselves in using our own potentials, we would deal with our life concerns—in whatever way was possible, as we saw above—rather readily. But the usual situation is not that simple. In various ways we block ourselves: We don't see all the factors in a situation, suppressing awareness of ways we contribute to them, displacing responsibility onto others, enacting old patterns that were more appropriate when we were younger. We experience ourselves as though we were less potent, more fragile or more externally constrained than is actually the case. We avoid direct confrontation of our concerns, put off dealing with painful issues, and deny ourselves full inner awareness. All the panoply of *defense mechanisms* that Freud and others have described may be operating to keep us from using our own powers to deal with our life concerns. (How ironic to call "defenses" what so cruelly make us vulnerable to hurt and disappointment!)

Essentially, these blocks to our full being are ways we misperceive our own natures or the situations in which our concerns are set. Such misperceptions come about because of experienced or threatened anxiety and pain and the conviction that if we open our awareness from its limitation we will in some fashion be catastrophically overcome. What that means is we are convinced we would be blown away, demolished, or wiped out if we didn't keep those blocks in place.

Beth remains in a frustrating, frightening, and seemingly hopeless marriage because she believes, at a level far below her conscious adult awareness, that she will be damned for eternity if she seeks a divorce.

Ted is continually irritable and unpleasant to be around. He constantly feels mistreated by others, and when friends try to give him feedback about how he comes across to them, Ted hears it as further abuse. He cannot afford to see how he's driven off relationships he deeply wants because he is convinced, although not consciously, that the pain of facing his responsibility would tear him open and destroy him.

Buck believes himself to be specially gifted, and indeed he is a person of very superior talents; but he produces very little. He complains unendingly of the limited vision of the people who edit the scientific journals or who have charge of research grants in his field, but repeatedly submits papers to the wrong journals and in a style which prevents their being acceptable. His research proposals tend to be sent in after the deadline and with only partial attention to the formal requirements of the agencies to which they are sent. Buck fears to see how self-defeating he needs to be in order to prevent the risk of defeat if he really puts himself on the line. He avoids fully entering competition in which his talents will be directly judged in comparisons with others. To

Buck the possibility of being found out as not special is equivalent to being killed, and in fact the identity he has cherished from his earliest years would be wiped out by such a disclosure.

These two postulations—that the basis for dealing with a life concern ultimately lies within the person having that concern and that that person is blocked from access to those resources—set the problem; they define the issue with which psychotherapy must deal. Our next postulations describe the basis for the work of psychotherapy.

Inward Searching: The Key to Life Concerns

Development of skill in subjective searching is the primary means by which one can overcome the blocks to access to one's own resources and thus deal most effectively with life concerns. It is surprising but absolutely true that most of us know very little about how to explore within our own subjectivity. This most primary of human skills, which is seldom taught directly by parents or teachers, is often handicapped or crippled by what is taught, and is seldom developed to any appreciable extent so that it can be turned to promptly when our life concerns require its employment. Recognition and development of this skill has importance, as we shall see, far beyond its application to the immediate concern that brings the person to therapy.

Well, what is this remarkable skill of inward searching? It is a set of attitudes and ways of being in one's consciousness, and when these are well used the resulting process is a more complete realization of our ultimate nature as subjective beings. This set of attitudes and skills is related to such more familiar experiences as meditation, creative thinking, prayer, contemplation, and problem solving; yet it is a unique process itself and particularly suited to the task of exploring concerns about life. Moreover, it is not, when fully understood, a new or contrived way of thinking. Rather, it is the very natural way the mind or the subjectivity of the person operates spontaneously when it is released from inhibition.

Inward searching is a process in which the awareness is tuned into one's own subjective experiencing in the moment and given free rein to move as it will, guided only by the sense of concern for one's life and the expectancy-intention of discovery. It is not self-consciousness self-examination or figuring things out. It is best when it is open, unforced, and almost playful.

This description is very brief, to be sure. In later pages we will elaborate on it.

The Process of Inward Searching

When a person describes the immediate inner experience of a life concern as fully as possible and with an expectancy of discovery, the inward searching process is set in motion. Searching is not some exotic art but is the simple process of using the less conscious resources of our human minds. When I am concerned about some part of my life, seriously involved with it and with the sense of possibility that it might be different, then I am "primed" and ready to use a talent as native to me as speech or walking, and one which like those two can be made more effective with guidance. Telling and retelling my concern, keeping open to whatever awarenesses present themselves as I talk, allowing my mind to "wander" (while keeping the underlying attitude of concerned expectancy), will bring me to continually fresh awarenesses.

> Tess at 27 has been married twice and divorced twice. She is now in love again and wanting to get married. Yet she feels great anxiety as her fiancé presses her to set a date. She comes to therapy convinced that somehow she has a jinx that makes her love relationships "go sour" and embarrassed to be so "superstitious." I'm going to give greatly abbreviated samples of her presentation of her concern.
>
> September 12th (intake):
>
> I know it's silly but I really do feel like I'm jinxed or something, like I'll never find a man I can really stay with. I don't know why I should feel that way; I've tried to think it all over, and there's just no reason.
>
> September 28th (5th interview):
>
> I know I'm just saying the same thing, but it really bugs me. I must do something that turns the man I'm with off, or at least that turned off my husbands. I feel like I'm my own worst enemy, but I can't see what it is I do.

December 4th (28th interview):

Well, I'll say it again if you think it will help, though you must be bored with hearing me go over this so many times. I mess up any relation in which I feel close to another person, especially a man. I don't mean to, but I get to feeling restless and trapped, and pretty soon . . . pretty soon I'm bitchy about little things. Hey, you know, I don't think I ever said that so directly before, did I?

February 10th (45th interview):

When Bill (fiancé) called I was angry. I felt like he was checking up on me or trying to tie me down. I started to tell him to lay off, that I wasn't his property, at least not yet. "Not yet!" That's what getting married means to me—and I think to a lot of men too. I'll be their property. Nuts to that! I'm going to belong to nobody but me.

May 9th (75th interview):

I know now that I don't have to belong to anyone. It's not like I'm a child, belonging to my parents. Still I can get very nasty sometimes when I feel people moving in too close. It's the same thing when I try to speak up in staff meetings. I'm always afraid somebody will steal my ideas, so I don't really put them out where anybody can see them. How'd I get this image of myself as such a frail little thing? You know, Jim, I'm not afraid; I can tangle with any of them. At least I can when I'm really with myself.

Important in this illustration is the way the definition of Tess's concern grew and deepened so that ultimately she is dealing with her whole way of seeing herself and her stance in her life. She is well on her way to the kind of emancipation from her past self-image that can make for true renewal in living.

What is perhaps not sufficiently evident in the example and discussion above is that the client—Tess or anyone else using this approach effectively—does *not* think up new ways of describing her concern; does not set out to solve the problem (of why she has trouble in relating to men); does not try to do anything other than to describe her concern as fully as possible at any given moment (and always with the attitude of concern and expectancy). Indeed, any attempts to solve problems, figure things out, tell the story in new ways, etc. is almost certain to be counter-productive. This is so because such attempts switch the client's focus and motivation from the concern itself to the form of its description or to the kind of impact it is having on the therapist; thus the powerful creative potential of involvement with one's own life issue is diluted or even diverted.

Disclosing the Blocks to Inward Searching

As the person describes the life concern again and again, the ways in which the free ranging of the searching awareness is blocked will be experienced and disclosed. This is a point which frequently surprises people who are unfamiliar with the way human intelligence works and who tend to think of human beings as though they were rather dull computers. If I ask a computer to read out the details of some recorded matter and then I ask it ten more times for the same information, I will receive ten exact copies of the material delivered on the first request. If I ask a human being to tell me about that same matter and then I ask for it to be repeated ten times, I will get eleven different presentations—unless the person has deliberately made himself into a machine by commiting the material to rote memory (from the same root as "rotation"—i.e., the basic wheel). (Try this experiment: Ask a friend to tell you about some incident; then ask him to retell it and compare the accounts.)

A human being, especially if telling something of genuine concern, almost literally *cannot* tell the same story twice in identical terms. The more open the person is to discovery in the process of the telling, the more the account will change with each telling. Thus theoretically, at least, a person who is able to allow awareness to range freely in any and all dimensions while exploring life concerns will soon begin to resolve those concerns in some manner. The expanding of awareness that comes about with continual, emotionally involved recounting of the concern opens up new possibilities of various kinds.

I say "theoretically" because none of us can let our awareness truly range freely in all dimensions. Instead, each of us in varying ways blocks, deflects, or distorts our inner searching. In the language of psychoanalysis these interferences with our inner searching are called *resistances,* and they are the patterns we have built up to protect ourselves from real or imagined threats. They continue to operate even when we do not consciously want them to do so, and that's the difficulty.

The resistances show themselves, first of all, as interferences with the searching process, as I've just said. Thus they intrude in the therapeutic interview and so disclose some of the source of the client's difficulty in using resources that are needed to resolve the concern. But the resistances are more than that. They also represent influences which make the client's life more cramped, unrewarding, and painful than it needs to be. The resistances, fully understood, are the ways in which we avoid the seemingly overwhelming anxieties of being human, such as the threat of death, the realization that we have but limited power and are vulnerable to chance, and the loneliness and separateness of being human. (Further discussion of the resistances will be found in Bugental, 1965, pp. 88–103; Fierman, 1965, pp. 15–64; and Reich, 1949, pp. 20–81.)

The Capacity for Inward Searching

A therapist facilitates the client's fullest use of the capacity for inward searching through (a) identifying the resistances which block the search process; (b) through insisting on the necessity of the client's being as fully and genuinely present as possible; and (c) through persistently taking the client and what the client says with complete seriousness.

What the therapist can and cannot do

I will talk about the functions which the therapist can perform for the client in a page or so, but first I want to make an important aside about that word "facilitates" in this postulation. To understand what is involved here, we must step back a bit and recognize that human beings always live in a paradox: We are inescapably and at once *a part of* yet *apart from* all other human beings. We can never wholly enter into another person's subjective world; neither can we ever completely be separate from any other person. (See Bugental, 1976; especially the accounts of Frank and Louise on pp. 101–189, to see how this paradox can profoundly affect the lives of people.)

Now back to that word, "facilitates." That word represents the very important but inexorably limited contribution which one person can make to another in the latter's efforts to remake or enrich life. That word reminds us of the limits to that contribution, limits which are inherent in the very nature of being human. The therapist can facilitate the client's searching but cannot do that job for the client. This is a point of fundamental importance, and it is one which a great many psychotherapists and psychoanalysts do not seem to understand: It is literally *impossible* for one person to give another insight into the latter person's inner life. Rogow (1970, p. 90) quotes an analyst as saying, "It's during the early months [of psychoanalysis] that there is the greatest challenge. You're trying to find out what the problem is, . . . You're like a sleuth trying to find out what happened. Maybe you can find out in six months, and the rest of the time you spend trying to get the patient to understand what you have found out."

This whodunit strain in much psychotherapy and psychoanalysis seeks a logical and coherent "interpretation" of the client's life and difficulties. Once it has been achieved, it is carefully taught to the client in the expectation that change or "cure" will result. The many people who have spent years in therapy and can talk endlessly about their childhood, their complexes, and their defenses—but who are not fundamentally changing to an enriched life experience—evidence the futility of second-hand "insight."

The nature of insight

Rightly understood, insight is like a dream. It is inner sight, seeing a vision within one's own being. Another's insight is irrevocably someone else's; it can never be one's own, and one's own can never be that other person's. The therapist who tries to give her or his client insight is attempting to be the eyes of a blind person—blind to the therapist's vision, but not blind within the client's own self. Such a therapist presumes too much, does not recognize or respect the ultimate autonomy of each person, is more apt to interfere with the client's inner vision than to facilitate it.

To get a more complete sense of the matter, try the following exercise.

> Imagine yourself waking in the morning from a rich, many dimensioned, and deeply involving dream. Struggling toward consciousness, you sense so much that preceded and ornamented the part of the dream which is still most vivid, but as you try to capture these other images you realize they are falling away into

irretrievable forgetting. Now, still drugged with sleep, you rouse your companion and begin telling the dream, hoping to preserve it by putting it into words. But there is so much that eludes the grasp of language; images that were so vital now twist and fragment; connections that seemed so significant drop apart. What you are able to convey is such a paltry and distorted residue of the once mind-filling imagery. Finally, if later you should hear your companion telling someone else of your dream—no matter how caringly and with what faithful attention to what you had reported—then you look on the mutilated remains of what once was so vital and rich.

Insight, rightly understood, is a product of inner sight, inner vision. It is not to be captured in words. Those who equate a verbal account of inner sight with the inward vision itself make the familiar semantic error of mistaking the map for the territory. What can be said about an inner sight is always less than the sight itself and is always relatively impotent in bringing about true life changes, especially when compared with the power of one's own liberating inward realization.

Inner sight is the birthright of each human being, but it is the hard-won attainment of those who commit themselves to the discipline of learning to use the inward-searching process. The wise psychotherapist can contribute significantly to that learning and takes pride in facilitating the client's autonomous powers. But the wise therapist knows no one can *give* a client insight.

Identifying the resistances

Here is where the therapist may play a most critically important role: identifying the interferences with the free ranging of the client's inner searching, displaying them to the client in such a way that their disabling effects are immediately experienced, and making evident the conviction that the client has other alternatives. The therapist doesn't accuse the client about the resistances or demand that they be relinquished. If truly dedicated to the client's sovereignty, the therapist is content persistently to bring to the client's awareness the fact of the resistances and all they mean in the client's life. This can be an exceedingly rough confrontation at times, and by my description I don't mean any passivity on the therapist's part. It is a highly skilled undertaking, calling for great sensitivity, discipline, and empathy.

When the client is brought to awareness of the self-crippling ways of being, when this recognition occurs repeatedly and in many contexts, when it is set in an atmosphere of caring and respect, and when the therapist genuinely communicates belief in the client's right to a self-chosen life, then the client almost always, sooner or later, moves toward getting free of the interferences, moves in the direction of greater wholeness and authenticity of being.

Insisting on the client's presence

In Chapter 3 I described the concept of *presence* and demonstrated why it is so important to the therapeutic process. The therapist's second basic function is calling on the client to be present, centered, life aware, talking *from* a sense of concern, rather than *about* a concern. This is actually but another facet of the disclosing of the resistances, but it is so important that it warrants separate discussion. The ways in which the client slides away from being centered are, of course, resistances equally. Clients are often inclined, particularly in the earlier stages of therapy, to be removed from themselves, trying to talk about their lives in a detached way as though they were objective observers, sometimes belittling or mocking their own feelings and impulses, sometimes being humorous or sarcastic about matters which are actually very emotionally important to them. For the therapist to join the client in attempting to carry out a searching effort under such circumstances is to engage in a charade which will have little likelihood of being productive in any way and very likely will ultimately prove counterproductive.

Taking the client seriously

The third function of the therapist in facilitating the client's inner searching process is to encourage and seriously attend to this person's telling of life concerns and all that comes with those accounts. This may seem a trivial or obvious matter; be assured it is not. Just as the client often resists engaging fully in the search process and avoids being fully centered, so the client is motivated on frequent occasions to try to draw the therapist away from fully being serious about what is going on. The client may protest the "somberness" of the proceedings, may try to make light of emotional distresses, may argue the work-orientation of the therapist, or may in other ways seek to avoid the relentless attention of the therapist.

To be sure, there are times when the sensitive therapist relaxes her or his constant focus on the client, but these are seldom the occasions when the client is attempting to escape the spotlight of that focus. A flexible and variable approach certainly sounds desirable, but "flexibility" and "variation" can be traps for the unwary facilitator who tries to prove responsiveness and ends up falling short of responsibility. For the most part the therapist needs to be alert, involved, and genuinely emotionally resonant to what the client is saying and how it is being presented. This is a sober, demanding, and immense task. It is serious, and the client will value the therapist's treating it so. Clients of mine have told me at the end of our long journey, "You know, one of the things you did that helped me most was that you took me seriously." So much for some of my vaunted interpretations of resistances and transferences; the attitude back of all that got over even more tellingly. And often these same clients had, at times, used every device they could muster to pull me away from that serious perspective.

Now I do not by any means intend to suggest that the therapeutic hours have no place for humor. Humor is often present, and I believe it is a trustworthy sign of a maturing therapeutic relationship and of the client's genuine progress when therapist and client can laugh unself-consciously together. This is seldom, if ever, a product of conscious intent to be funny on the part of either but grows out of their serious and nearly total involvement with the task at hand.

Respect and Genuine Caring: Essentials to the Relationship

A relation of mutual respect and genuine caring is the ideal medium in which this facilitating process can occur and in which the searching can be best forwarded. In a most fundamental way, the relation of client and therapist is, or needs to be, the most real relationship of the client's life. It is only in an atmosphere of commitment to authenticity that one can risk the sort of nakedness of self-disclosure that is essential to thoroughgoing inner search. This is not a one-sided intimacy, but one which can only be fostered for the client if the therapist is similarly committed to being as fully present as possible.

The facilitator's wisdom is not essential to this enterprise. It is a good thing, an enriching contribution to the process. It is not critical that it be matured; time and experience will increase it. The therapist's skills may or may not be critically important. There are in many clients' therapeutic courses, junctures at which skill may make a vital difference, but ultimately skill is of secondary significance.

What is primary, indeed essential (although not sufficient), is the attitude of the therapist. This must be compounded of respect for the client and for the client's ultimate autonomy, belief in the growth potential of the human being and the potency of the searching process to actualize that growth, and readiness to commit oneself to perservering with the client, keeping faith through provocation, temptation, and weariness.

We have now seen the preconditions for intensive psychotherapy and the vehicles through which the work of that therapy is accomplished. It remains only to make a simple statement of the outcome to be expected from this enterprise.

The Yield from Inward Searching

The person who explores life concerns in this fashion and utilizes the awareness that the search process yields, will emerge with a changed and enlarged sense of identity and power. Take note that this postulate does not say, "all problems solved," "living more happily," "more friends," "greater success in work," "sexually a better lover," "able to influence people readily," or any other such desired and desirable outcomes, although most all of these are sought, consciously or not, by a lot of people who begin therapy.

Intensive psychotherapy of the sort discussed in this book is not a problem-solving technique. Not infrequently, the client at the end of several years of hard, costly, demanding work will recognize, "I still have the same hang-up I had when I came, but somehow it seems different now, smaller, less threatening. It's like it's remained the same, but I've grown much larger, so it doesn't seem so important or bothersome any more."

"I've grown much larger." That is one of the most important products of this kind of work. The client who carries through with a therapist who is genuinely present will almost always experience more potential, more power, more choices, more hope, and more sureness in inner being. These are considerable gains to be sure, but

they are not the magical ones so many people originally and often secretly sought.

And having the same hang-ups really doesn't mean being in the same distress. Quite to the contrary, the client making such a statement often is expressing a changed feeling about having hang-ups, a greater appreciation of patterns that serve well at times and interfere at others, a sense of perspective about one's own being that is less continually evaluative and more frequently at one and at ease.

5

The Travelers Form a Bond and Begin Their Journey: The Relationship and Processes of Psychotherapy

The preliminaries largely over, the journey begins. The travelers embark, the vessel moves, and the familiar world fades—more quickly to the eye, more slowly to the mind, but in either case inexorably dropping behind as the venture establishes its own rhythms. Always the trip is changing as it goes; the best plans are the plans that can readily be adapted to answer the questions put by the opportunities or necessities of actuality. The traveler seeks sure guidance, guarantees of safe passage, but the guide offers only the suppositions of experience—valuable experience but always other experiences than those of this particular road on this unique day.

One can make generalizations about psychotherapy—the libraries are full of them, and I'm adding to the supply right now—but no single actual therapeutic course ever fits the pattern all along the line. It is useful, however, to have a general itinerary in mind; then variations from it tend to be more meaningful and rewarding. Essential to the process, of course, is the relationship that client and therapist grow between them. The therapist has a general set toward the kind of working partnership felt to be most fruitful; yet experience has taught that the client will strongly if unconsciously influence the way the actual relationship evolves. Each such team configuration is unique. That is at once the fascination and opportunity of this work and often its complication and frustration as well.

Conceptualizing the Ideal Therapeutic Partnership

Two people enter into a partnership from which both hope for important returns. The enterprise is the exploration of the inner world of one partner, and the outcome, if all goes well, will be the revitalization of that person's life. That renewal may range from the trivial to the profound, from relief of discomfort for a time to a complete change of the way the client lives and is in the world, from a limited benefit to the client alone to a change so pervasive that all who are involved with the client subsequently experience from such encounters a different consequence than would otherwise have occurred.

But the other partner, the therapist, brings important contributions to the task and reaps significant renewal for living as well, a gain which includes the sense of having participated in an incomparably meaningful venture.

In addition, when things go well both partners obtain quite practical products. For one, these may be increased effectiveness and satisfaction in daily activities and relationships; for the other, the returns often include finances important to livelihood. For these, and as a part of the professional commitment, the therapist-partner intends to give the other's needs important degrees of priority whenever these needs conflict with the therapist's own personal concerns. But the professional knows, too, that in that way both will ultimately experience most from the undertaking.

And truth to tell, many times the partners—sometimes one, more often both—are drawn on from day to day by the sheer adventure of their work and the sense of sharing deeply, despite the inevitable dry spells. Such is the unique human enterprise called *intensive psychotherapy.* We need to think now about the client-therapist relationship through which this pursuit is carried into effect.

An Array of Models of the Therapeutic Relationship

The good parent

Although it likely few would admit it in so many words, there are many therapists today who play this role which was deemed enlightened more than a century ago (Bockoven, 1963). They are to be identified by their autocratic direction of their clients, their unquestioning assumption that they know better what the clients should do than do those clients themselves, and by their holding apart from real engagement on anything like equal terms with their clients.

Psuedo-equality

In contrast is the conception that "we're all just the same and there's no basis for someone to be in any special role as therapist unless that person is hung-up on status needs." This approach to the relationship tends to belittle theory, technique, responsibility, and most everything except just letting it all hang out. One needs to be nimble to get any attention to the client's concerns because the nontherapist has had a lot more practice in grabbing air time to do her or his thing.

Psychoanalytic blank screen

In contrast to both of the foregoing models, the classical psychoanalytic ideal is one which emphasizes the psychological invisibility of the therapist. The analyst's task is to be as unself-disclosing as possible so that whatever the client may report experiencing about the therapist's attitudes, emotions, or opinions can be flatly interpreted as projection—i.e., coming from some inner concern of the client. An admirable conception, and one in keeping with the nineteenth century ideal of complete objectivity. Unfortunately, it is a complete impossibility.

Participant observer

Harry Stack Sullivan (1947) broke with the psychoanalytic tradition of the blank screen, insisting that the therapist was always a part of whatever transpired in the consulting room, that the client's reactions were in some part stimulated by whatever the analyst did, and that the therapist was cut off from important data by refusing to recognize involvement in this interactive process. Sullivan's argument was part of his whole stand which insisted that Freud overemphasized the biological and instinctive, giving too little attention to the experiential and social. It is an interesting footnote that Sullivan himself is often described as cold and aloof, relatively unresponsive. Clearly he meant a mild departure from the classical position.

The congruent mirror

Carl R. Rogers (1942, 1951, 1961) is one of the few who are totally American who have had a pervasive impact on the field of psychotherapy. Consistently he advances his conviction that human beings are essentially good and to be trusted, that they have the potential to heal themselves, and that honest relationships are the major force for change and betterment in human affairs. In his own life, as well, this man has sought to live what he taught so well to so many.

In Rogers' view the ideal therapeutic relationship is characterized by *congruence.* This term is used to characterize state of being of a person in which what one experiences within (e.g., sympathy, annoyance, surprise) while listening to the client is also what the person is aware of in consciousness and is likewise what is expressed to the client. Such congruence in the therapist, Rogers feels (and I fully agree), is a powerful influence in aiding the client to become more congruent and whole.

The other aspect of the therapist's task in this view is that of mirroring back to the client as accurately as possible what it is that the therapist hears the client saying. This is a deceptively demanding undertaking for it requires that the therapist avoid any interpretation, teaching, suggestions, evaluations, support, guidance, or other intrusion. Instead, the therapist seeks to understand the client's experience and reflect it back so that the latter may bring the healing/growth potential to focus in self-renewal.

The director-interactor
A new model for the therapist calls for that person to function in two ways with the client. First, the therapist is a resource for activities which may facilitate the client's exploring inner experience; and second, the therapist uses personal reactions to the client as data for their interaction. Such therapists are often practitioners of the action therapies, as described in the first chapter and as such are very active in the therapeutic exchange, suggesting things for the client to do, speaking for the repressed parts of the client, taunting and encouraging, and in many other ways involving themselves in the interplay.

An Existential-humanistic Ideal for the Client-therapist Relationship

The ideal relationship for client and therapist is the one which will most facilitate client inner exploration, in my view. Just what the characteristics of such a relationship will be varies with the particular client, the point in the client's life at which the therapy is taking place, the kinds of issues the client is confronting, the kind of person the therapist is, the evolution of their relationship up to this point, and the competing influences going on in the client's extra-therapy life, as well as other influences.

In short, it is not possible to write a general prescription for the sort of client-therapist relationship which is ideal. What is possible is to describe some of the important characteristics of such relations and to indicate some of the significance of those qualities.

Mutuality
Each of the things I'll say about the therapeutic relationship in the following paragraphs needs to be understood as having the adjective "mutual" solidly attached to it. I believe that the partners in this enterprise must sense that they share a common bond which is greater than any particulars of their differences. This is the bond of being human, of being incomplete, of being subject to fate and frustrations, of seeking to have good lives, of caring about what

happens. This foundation is easily taken for granted, but must not be assumed too casually. Often implicitly and not infrequently explicitly, one or the other participant will refer to and draw strength from that rock-bottom sharedness.

To say that the therapeutic collaborators share much is not, however, to say that there are no differences between them. They are not the same in what they bring to their meetings, in what they need to do while there, or in what they hope to realize from these sessions. To be sure, there is in each of these regards much that is similar still, but similarity should not be mistaken for sameness.

The good therapeutic relationship usually starts with the differences between the partners quite marked and, if all goes well, it may end with those differences largely transcended. Indeed, in a few of my relationships with clients who were themselves therapists, it proved desirable to reverse our roles for a time near or after the end of our formal therapist-client work together.

Honesty

Both participants in this enterprise need to work toward being as fully straight with themselves and each other as they can possibly be. This is often hard for both. The client will, in a large percentage of the times, deceive, withhold, or distort some things. Far from being something "bad" that the client is doing, however, such inevitable deceptions can provide important material as they are disclosed and client and therapist jointly inquire into the need for such self-defeating actions.

The therapist too will know temptations to dissemble on occasion. Often these take the form of giving the impression of knowing, remembering, or perceiving more than one actually does. Subtly or obviously, the therapist may claim expertise not actually possessed or may portray or express a freedom from personal distress more hoped for than achieved. It is so easy to slide into these, and most of us do on occasion. Just as with the client, the therapist needs to avoid self-censure for such lapses. Instead these can be jumping off points for inner inquiry—seeking the help of another professional if indicated—to deal with the lack of self-acceptance thus disclosed.

This is more than a point of fairness or even of moral appropriateness, although these are not minor considerations. The significance is deeper: the client in a very real way must depend on the therapist as a source of validation for perceptions. Thus the blank screen therapist importantly misleads the client when all patient perceptions of the therapist are deemed projections. The client must be able to trust that the therapist will attempt to be as honest as possible in response. This does not mean, necessarily, that the therapist will answer any and all questions, but that what the therapist does say will be as straightforward as it is possible to make it.

CL-1: I had the feeling just then that I was irritating you by my questions.
TH-1: Yes, I guess that's right. I know I felt kind of edgy when you kept on pressing me.
CL-2: Why was that?
TH-2: It has to do with something in your manner which suggests you find a delight in pursuing me, and it comes also from some things in my own history which make me more than usually sensitive about being teased.
CL-3: What happened to you to make you sensitive that way?
TH-3: I really don't think it would be useful to your therapy for me to go into those experiences now. Another time, we might talk about them. For now, I think it would be most helpful for you to see what your feelings may be about me and about our exchange right now.

Each of the responses above is, to my mind, honest and mutual in what it expresses of the relationship between this therapist and this client. It is my assumption that the therapist in TH-3 is not using some maneuver to avoid an uncomfortable question, but is genuinely trying to keep a working focus on the issue of the client's own inner experience rather than yielding to the invitation to digress.

Respect

Throughout the relationship, an attitude of mutual respect is essential. This means that the therapist acts in a way which is consistent with the fundamental gravity of the task to which the partners have set themselves. This does not mean that there is no place for lightness, humor, or playfulness in the therapeutic process. If the last two sentences seem contradictory, consider how often you've turned away from a television program replete with laugh-track humor with a vague feeling of having been cheated or of having a flat taste in your mouth where the trumped-up laugh was a minute before. Genuine humor—or lightness or play—comes out of a deeper fountain of being in touch with the paradoxes and surprises of life.

An attitude of respect implies that there is a dignity to the role of being a client seeking to reexamine one's life and to direct it toward more meaningful and satisfying outcomes—and that there is a wholesome pride in being chosen to accompany someone on such a quest. It means that both participants take very seriously their parts in what goes on, and that the therapy has a high priority among competing concerns in both of their lives. Neither will lightly cancel or be late for their meetings; nor will either casually discuss in other settings what transpires between them.

Respect means that both client and therapist recognize and commit themselves to the fact that in a very real way they are engaged in a struggle with death for the life of one or both of them. The death of vitality, of possibility, of hope, of actualizing one's potential is a very real tragedy, and its reversal is a genuine triumph for the human spirit.

Dynamic

The ideal therapeutic relationship is continually evolving and changing. It is not a way of being together, which is established early in the participants' relation and remains unchanged; instead it is constantly changing as the work progresses and as the needs of the participants emerge. At one point, the therapist may be relatively passive and concentrating solely on demonstrating understanding and acceptance; at other times, it will be appropriate to be highly active, confronting, and persistent. At some points the client will look for guidance or support; while at other times the need may be to challenge any lead from the therapist and to insist on one's own way of proceeding. A good therapeutic relationship, to my mind, is not specifiable in general or in the abstract. It is flexible, unique in important ways to the two participants at any given time. The same therapist will have a different relationship with each individual client and the same client would have a different relationship with another therapist.

Vital

The word "vital " has to do with the fact of life itself. Such is the focus of the work of the therapeutic partners. This significance has already been alluded to above, but it has further implications which I want to draw out here. I believe that human life is a far richer, deeper, more ineffable, less understood phenomenon than we ever fully appreciate. It is necessary—even essential—to much of the supporting apparatus of life (e.g., society, security, peaceful relations among people) to have some constraints on what we do (folkways, laws), but we should not confuse those practical necessities with the natural limits of the human condition. Psychotherapy, to my mind, must often be at the frontier between the accepted (the conventional) and the unconventional or even the outright forbidden.

What this means is that depth psychotherapy, which seeks to aid the client in getting in touch with the very roots of being in life, will often be a risky and socially questionable undertaking. This is a point often misunderstood by those who have only an abstract knowledge of what is involved in intensive, life-changing psychotherapy. Such work deals with the sources of violence, murder, suicide, rape, crime, brutality, sacrilege, wanton destruction, and other impulses and actions that civilizations and intelligent people abhor. Many people will recognize this, albeit often reluctantly, but they insist that the therapy need only talk about such possibilities but need not get beyond the relatively abstract level.

Such a view of human nature is naive at best and too often consciously self-blinding. The line between action and subjective impulse is not that clear-cut nor so easily maintained. Depth psychotherapy must often hover at or on both sides of that uneasy and hazardous border. Only when the undomesticated feelings and yearnings that are part of all of us are allowed to emerge and find some expression, hopefully a somewhat controlled and muted one, is there the possibility of such genuine working through that the client can live with inner and outer balance and without imposing energy-sapping self-policing controls.

Trusting

This is a point on which the humanistic view of man is at rather marked contrast with many other perspectives. For Freud, man's impulses toward sexuality and aggression were so ultimately destructive that only through the constraints of society and the maturation of self-control and sublimation could he see any way of protecting ourselves against ourselves. Traditional religious views have similarily sought to capture and cage the wild beast within us, and much of the apparatus of our culture today still is founded on a mistrust of human impulses.

The humanistic stance is that when human beings are given trust, when they are helped to confront all of their feelings and impulses in an atmosphere that is not judgmental, and when they have an opportunity to weigh alternatives without premature pressure to act, then, and only then, can human beings be relieved of the age-old fear of their own nature and begin to live as whole persons, and then, and only then, will they work out ways to heighten the synergy in which they live with their fellows.

This is a hypothesis about the nature of human life which is radically at odds with that by which men and women have lived for most of their history so far as we know it. For individuals who have journeyed to the further therapeutic levels I've described, I can attest that without exception they bear out this trust. But it is equally true that this is an extremely minute sampling and that even when compounded by all the other clients of other therapists who have gone through similar processes—and we don't know that all would report such results—the quantity is still exceedingly small. Nevertheless, I and other humanistic psychologists argue that the bankruptcy of the old view of human nature is so manifest around us that we must seek some truly revolutionary new perspective. At least, we maintain, ours has some empirical footing and deserves consideration.

Let me be clear about one frequent misunderstanding: What I argue for is *not* a dropping of all control on human impulses and action. If depth psychotherapy has taught me anything it is that we are all capable of enormities of all kinds (Bugental, 1974). Simply loosing the shackles of convention and law would be madness, and much that is happening in our culture now demonstrates that. What I advocate is a sincere and widespread effort to revise the guiding image of our own natures which we carry with us into every phase of life. (Bugental, 1971, describes this proposal further.)

Phases in the Psychotherapeutic Process

I want to describe the way intensive psychotherapy may advance toward helping the client claim inner vision and increased vitality.

To write such a description I will abstract and objectify what is essentially a very concrete and subjective process. The living transactions which are the vital struggles of the therapeutic partners undergo some inevitable distortions when we reduce them to linear words and sentences, just as an X-ray is a distortion if taken to represent a living person.

Yet an X-ray can be a valuable aid to understanding the functioning of the total person. It eliminates certain features to highlight others. Those aspects set aside are not less important necessarily; they are only dispensable for a particular and limited purpose. The skeletal system may for a period be studied without reference to the circulatory or the neural, but one does well always to keep peripherally aware of those other vital aspects if one is to understand the whole body or the real person. Indeed, if one is to seek a full understanding of the skeletal system, it must be in such a way that its relation to all other systems and to the whole is continually kept in mind.

Beginning the Development of an Alliance

The relationship which I have with my client is an essential element of the entire process. If all goes well, it will be the bridge over which the client will travel from a present way of life to a reborn way of being. It will have to provide support in times of enthusiasm and times of despair, in periods of struggle and conflict and through the dark days when the client may need to attack the bridge itself and me as well. As we have seen, this relationship is not immediately comparable to any other in life. It is a friendship; it is a love affair; it is a partnership; it is a blood bond; it is a duel; it is all of these and none of them and yet something more. It is a *therapeutic alliance,* a bond between what is best and most dedicated in the therapist and what is most health-seeking and courageous in the client. It will have many other elements in it at various points, but this is its essence. Each partner to the alliance will fall short at times of being all that it demands and yet it must endure.

The early sessions of the therapy are taken up with the obvious business of getting acquainted, but in that familiar process I have some unfamiliar intents. I want to find out as soon as possible what are the most available resources within the client which motivate for growth. These may be dreams and hopes for oneself, a sensing of something far more that might be the taste of living, treasured memories of peak experiences and moments of unusual clarity of vision (when inner sensing was unusually aware). But there will also be the private and terrible agonies of self-betrayals, of despair for one's life, of failures in relations and in actions, of feeling trapped in futile repetitions. I will have need of all I can learn of what powers the client's seeking for change, relief, opportunity, or growth. These will be the bridge members upon which the journey, perhaps even literal life, will depend.

Arousing and Focusing the Client's Motivation to have Centered Awareness of Being

Usually the client comes to therapy seeking relief of some distress—experiences of panic, inability to work up to capacity, uncontrolled angry episodes. It is unusual for the client to recognize how crippled the inner awareness is or to sense how important that subjective sensing is to the relief of distress. Thus an early necessity in the therapist's work is to link up the client's concern over the presenting symptom with the more significant underlying condition. Gradually, after the therapist has many times conveyed the belief that the client is importantly handicapped in self-guiding, the latter will begin to sense a need to have a fuller capacity for self-knowing. Then will come instances in which briefly the client gets such awareness, and now the therapist can strongly underscore the difference this makes in client's life. Ideally, the two can then become full partners in pursuing this needed facility, and thus the fundamental therapeutic work can go forward.

Disclosing and Working through Resistances

In the last chapter, I described how our native, inner-searching process becomes blocked for a variety of reasons. The resistances which impede that search were necessary to the client at some prior point in life; they may or may not be experienced as so essential today. A major amount of the therapeutic work is involved in identifying, disclosing, and working through these resistances.

A common-sensical rule-of-thumb which I and other therapists use to some extent is to go through three steps in this process. First is the identification of the resistance pattern as it is displayed in the therapeutic hour ("You seem to keep everything on a very abstract, intellectual level when you talk about the conflict with your son"). Repeatedly the therapist watches for and points to a particular pattern of resisting full open awareness with emotional involvement. After a time, hopefully, the client begins to recognize the pattern spontaneously ("I can hear myself getting abstract now as I think of Tim").

Now the therapist moves to the second step, continuing to point to the pattern if the client does not do so. This next phase involves pointing out that the client must have some purpose in continuing this way of self-blocking ("You must need to keep control carefully when you think about Tim" or "You have surely had your reasons for staying kind of distant when you're dealing with how Tim affects you"). Often, with a well-motivated client, this will encourage seeking for what may be the source of the resistance pattern. In any case, as soon as it is clear that the client recognizes the resistance as being or having been useful, the discovery of the underlying function begins ("If I let my feelings out, I might be too hard on him" or "I've learned I can't think clearly when I let go to my emotions"). Now, whenever the client exhibits the resistance pattern, the therapist is apt to say, "You must feel anxious about your feelings and where they'll take you since you've just become very abstract and detached in the way you talk."

Working through the layers of the resistance

This work of identifying and disclosing the roots of the resistance is one of the major phases of intensive, thoroughgoing psychotherapy. It is usually the most time-consuming and demanding phase of the work as well. It is sometimes referred to as *peeling the onion,* as therapist and client expose and make it possible for the latter to relinquish one resistance after another.

> Kate was a distant and forbidding woman when she first came to therapy. She sought to treat herself as impersonally as she treated everyone else. As the first layer of her resistance—her refusal to yield to the emotional involvement in telling about her life—was disclosed and worked through, she began to talk about having emotional experiences, but she attempted to do so with

clinical detachment. In turn, this layer was identified and gave way to a period of excessive optimism, which was yet another way of warding off free and open inner exploration (and the recognition that she was subject to contingency and disappointment).

Thus the work of client and therapist is that of freeing the former's awareness of encumbering armor and padding, all of which have at some time served the client to prevent what seemed overwhelming pain or outright destruction. This process is relatively simple to describe, but is one of great subtlety and variety in the actual therapeutic situation. It must be gone through repeatedly, with many changes and nuances. The necessity is to demonstrate over and over again in ways such that the client deeply experiences, rather than simply cognitively recognizes, how pervasive are the patterns through which living is crippled and how crippled indeed it is. This working through is essential to forestall an intellectualized short-circuiting of the growth process, to provide sufficient motivation to carry the client through some of the very painful and frightening work yet to be done, and to ensure as broad and centered awareness as possible. (See Bugental, 1976, for examples in detail of the resistances and their resolution through therapeutic confrontations.)

Confronting Existential Anxiety

If the partners have been steadfast and effective in their work to this point, they are likely arriving at the brink of the most demanding phase of the entire therapeutic process. This is the point at which the more evocative therapeutic levels (which I termed emancipation and transcendence in the first chapter) become possibilities, and thus it is also the point at which some clients and therapists turn back from pressing further.

The therapeutic task when the resistances have been in some appreciable degree confronted and worked through becomes that of supporting the client in a journey into and through hell. That sounds very melodramatic, but it is by no means an exaggeration. If the client chooses to continue the search for greater authenticity in being, for more freedom from the constrains of the "self" as a way of being defined, for experiencing the transpersonal possibilities of consciousness, then the client chooses the route that leads through dread, despair, and nothingness. This hell is composed of the client's most terrifying, and heretofore suppressed and repressed, terrors about life. The client must fight demons which are the denied visions of his or her own nature and the frightening realities of the world. Only by persevering through these agonies can the client achieve such a renewal of being that patterns which have structured life till that point can be discarded.

One may sense a parallel to the sagas of quests and heroic journeys, as diverse as the Odyssey, the Hobbit stories, or many others. This literary form is certainly as old as human nature, and the parallel is no happenstance. Such stories express our common and largely unconscious yearning to conquer those forces within ourselves which keep us from our rightful sovereignty within our own lives.

In more concrete terms, the client must begin to let go of the defenses, which have for so long seemed essential—a record of achievements, insistence on fairness, a continual angry detachment, the need to please, a stance of objectivity, unwillingness to change, the unrelenting effort to know and do everything—and thus the client experiences the very anxiety these defenses have held off. Eventually one comes to the underlying conditions of being human, to those sources of existential anxiety which cannot be explained or analyzed away, to death and relentless change, to the emptiness of the Void, to responsibility and choice, to our separateness which yet involves us inexorably with others, to guilt and limitedness, and to omnipresent and potentially overwhelming contingency. (In another place—Bugental, 1965, Parts 1 and 3—I have set forth my view of the nature of being, of the existential confrontations which cannot be analyzed away, and of the significance for personal actualization which is potential).

I introduced this phase of the work by speaking of the client facing a journey through hell. Now, perhaps, it will be clear why this is no exaggeration. The searching process facilitated by the disclosure and gradual relinquishment of the resistances inexorably moves from the superficial to the most central life concerns. In this way each client moves toward facing personal and unique terrors. This is no descent into a Milton's conception of torment. It is rather the confrontation with what each of us most dreads and has longest held apart from conscious awareness. It is veritable hell, tailored to the individual.

The existential crisis

The working through of the resistances brings about the dreaded confrontation with existential anxiety, and imperceptibly both move the client to the brink of the crisis of existence. This *night journey, dark night of the soul,* or *confrontation with the Void* seems to occur in some form and with some degree of extremity in many but not all of the therapeutic courses in which I have had a part.

The existential crisis is an encounter with death. Almost always the client finds death images and impulses coming unbidden into consciousness. Thoughts of suicide, and sometimes even suicidal actions, may occur. Less frequently homicidal impulses, usually directed toward parents or parental figures, surface. And there is a murder-suicide to be done. This is a figure of speech only to the extent that the client survives physically and in most basic character structure. What must die are the ways the client has given substance to being and to the world. For the person in this house of death, that is only an academic distinction, for one feels oneself on the brink of dissolution and the world on the verge of destruction. And indeed one's *self,* as I have defined that concept on pp. 10 and 132, is dying, at least as a basis for the sense of personal identity.

I will not attempt to detail all that is involved in bringing a person to this perilous juncture nor the many considerations the therapist must keep in mind in standing by the client through this time (see Bugental, 1965, Chapter 10). Instead I will sketch out a representative and frequently central element in the evolution to and through the crisis.

As we saw in the first chapter, Karen Horney (1950) has described the way many, if not most, people in our culture develop and live in terms of two alienated images of themselves. These she calls the *idealized image* and the *despised image.* The idealized image one has is a secret idea of the remarkable person one would be *if only* one were all that is sensed as deep down potential. Founded on the realistic awareness of how much of that potential is largely untapped, this exaggerated notion grows by disregarding all limitations, all interferences of environment, all conflicts within oneself, all but the most inviting intimations of superiority. Conversely, the despised image feeds on fears of the sort of person one dreads being discovered to be. It develops out of all the little and big secrets of deceptions, failures, and violent and obscene impulses. It ignores any extenuation, any comparisons that might be reassuring, any gains in perceptiveness or self-direction, as it festers and grows in nightmare fashion.

Both of these alienated images are set in contrast to the beingness of the client, to human fallibility and strengths, to vulnerability to circumstance, and to perseverence and courage. Both images function at less than fully conscious levels and operate to obscure realistic awareness of one's actual way of being in the world. The idealized image is a picture of perfection, of nearly divine power, of universal attractiveness, and because it is so extreme it tends to rob realistic attainments of their savor and to undermine efforts to achieve what can be reached. The despised image is a portrait of darkest vileness, of irredeemable evil in which any hint of caring or worth is seen only as hypocrisy and any worthy act is but a fluke. Because it is thus exaggerated, the person tends to engage in orgies of self-loathing, periods of hopelessness, and impulses toward destructiveness of self and all else.

As the work of therapy progresses and the resistances are peeled back, there is repeated and often painful recognition of how much energy has gone into efforts to achieve an impossible perfection and to disguise and flee from an exaggerated vileness. Patterns vary from person to person, but often it is the idealized image that is longest kept a treasured secret; while the despised image is slowly, agonizingly brought to light. Anxiously, expecting ultimate rejection at every disclosure, the client brings forth shameful admissions, guilty thoughts and acts, perverse and obscene impulses, and all the sad and destructive cargo of self-hate. Often the very process of airing all this is itself a healing one, but the therapist does well to be cautious of quick reassurances or apparent casualness to what is being disclosed. Unless the client feels deeply that the gravity and wrongness of what is displayed is truly recognized, there can be no full discharge of this ghastly burden.

There is a hidden reason is this. All of the specifics of thought, feeling, word, and deed, as shocking as they are to the client and may be to a lesser extent to the therapist, are but the surface aspects of what is felt to be indescribably more repugnant. That ultimate abhorence is felt by the client in so many cases as something beyond specification, back of any particulars. In its deepest reach, it is the client's primal feeling of intrinsic unacceptability, which no words can express nor any absolution redeem. Only the process of inner searching, of open disclosure, and of wordless recognition and acceptance can bring solace to this wound.

It is difficult to convey in a relatively cool manner in a book how abject is this conviction of ultimate worthlessness. Suffice it to say that people who confront it under less therapeutic circumstances than those I'm trying to set forth may be impelled to the acts of horror and violence which our news media so diligently detail, and which we so unwillingly but fascinatedly read (see Bugental, 1974). Killing oneself is often an impulse to keep control of what seems an otherwise unconquerable evil which is threatening to erupt out of one's depths. Thus suicide may be a way of trying to preserve a better self or to protect others.

To recapitulate: In the existential crisis, the client comes to face that both of these alienated images are substitutes for being in one's own life, that each serves to displace the immediacy of experience, and only by relinquishing them can one step forth naked and direct into living. But there is a fearful wrenching involved in that relinquishment. That nakedness seems, and indeed is, so terribly vulnerable and so truly mortal. Usually the actual "killing" of the old self (with the idealized and despised images implicit within it) occurs in some kind of break-out experience. In a very real sense, the client must go out of control for at least a brief period because the ways on which control has previously depended have been bound up with old patterns of being. Until they are truly let go of, they cannot be replaced.

Therapist's control

There is a further and important part of this going out of control which I have come to believe to be important but which is not usually noted in the professional literature. I will not try to elaborate on it here, but I am increasingly convinced that it too is essential. I think the therapist as well must let go of control, at least in some part or some ways, for an interval. If the client consciously or unconsciously lets go of control trusting that in the background the therapist has full control, then the client has not really made the full leap of faith to a new way of being, but has tried to cross over using the bridge of the therapist's control. In short, I believe that the most meaningful leap of faith a person can make is that in which one jumps knowing only that in that moment one is the jumper and without any promise of where one will land or any hope of the potential saving intervention of the therapist's power.

The therapist cannot go out of control by intent. That would be a parody of a dynamic human process. It is only meaningful when the professional's deep participation in the struggle brings it about. Further, this observation is no warrant for the unbridled impulsivity on the part of the therapist. Quite the contrary, it seems to me to impose greater demands to be aware, synergically attuned, and deeply present with the client. (See Farber, 1966, Chapter 8 for a related conception.)

Supporting New Learning and New Ways of Being

People seem to vary widely in their need for a period of trying out new patterns of having their lives. Some profit from a kind of coaching support in which they try out new ways of relating to other people, are helped to rethink what they experience in fresh terms. For example, Kate gained much from talking over her changed interaction with others and reminding herself that conflict did not signal the end of relationship and that change might mean opportunity as much as loss. Others seem to move out from formal therapy rather promptly after the crisis is past and to find other settings in which to continue their growth.

Involved in this process is the transfer of reinforcing power back to the client from the therapist in whom it has been invested for some time. This may mean working out some of the residuals of the expectations of magical changes with which many of us entered our therapy. It certainly entails learning to trust the subjective life in place of the former reliance on that which was objective and public.

Mourning

One of the most poignant processes and important functions of this period for many people is the grief work of mourning for the life that might have been but can never be. Many clients, and I myself, say something like, "Oh God, if I'd only known sooner, if I'd only found out ten (20 or 30) years ago that I didn't have to fight myself so." The recognition of the fullness of life that is now possible cannot but have implications for the impoverished living that has been true before. And it is essential that well-meaning reassurance not rob the patient of having this grief. It frees the person to know new vitality fully. Here too, therapeutic groups can be very meaningful vehicles to this task.

Separating

Finally there is the task of separation from the therapist. The long journey has come to a new phase and the client must go on with new companions. Sometimes there is an important work to be accomplished in dealing with the client's anger at the therapist, anger which has been held in check to this point. When this occurs, the separation phase may be prolonged. The anger seems to arise from one or more of several interrelated sources: disillusionment with the therapist who is now discovered to be fallible and inadequate in ways that formerly seemed invisible, the wish for a continuing or more intimate relationship with the therapist than the latter can welcome genuinely, or the negative transference (the projection of elements of the despised self on the therapist just as the idealized image was formerly so projected).

The process of working through this termination anger is essentially the same as has been described for dealing with other resistances to accepting one's real situation in life. The most important difference is that here the therapist needs to gird up courage and be as authentic as possible. This often means that the therapist will be more self-disclosing than previously, but that is not the necessary or only implication.

6

The Traveler Discovers the Rewards and Hazards of the Journey: The Main Phases of the Course of Therapy—Client's Perspective

The traveler and the guide—each has a part in the processes of the journey; each needs the other to give meaning, form, and fullness to the enterprise. The guide overtly as well as less obviously instructs, and the traveler learns. The traveler teaches also, and the wise guide both learns how to aid the client and learns from the client as well. In this exchange the traveler begins to be changed; by persevering through the hardships and relishing the delights, the traveler is becoming a different person. The sensitivities and skills of the journey become lasting parts of the traveler, parts which will be retained long after the trip is over.

It is time to describe the central process through which the work of psychotherapy is accomplished. This is a skill which the client must learn to value, to use effectively, and to make an intrinsic part of the way of being. This skill is that of mobilizing and directing intentionality in inward searching. The potential for this skill, even some measure of effectiveness in using it, is present in every person, but it is inadequately developed or appreciated by most people. The client who comes fully to grasp and value this process makes a gain which is life-wide and life-long.

In learning to use this process, the client goes through the experiences and confronts the issues which are essential to therapeutic change and growth. Thus the possibilities of life are opened up to the client through coming to appreciate and use latent capacities more fully.

Focusing Intentionality in Inward Searching

The client comes to psychotherapy seeking relief from distress—from pain or anxiety or from the sense of missing the possibilities life has to offer. The client, by the very act of coming to therapy, demonstrates a step taken that many others experiencing similar pain or anxiety, a similar sense of unfilled potential, have not taken. That crucially different step is the mobilization of concern for one's life and the determination to do something about it. This process may be called *intention. Intentionality* is one of the distinguishing characteristics of human beings.

Intentionality

The intentionality of the person is a fundamental aspect of subjectivity. It makes possible the directionality of the person, gives rise to an image of the life the person seeks to bring into being. Rollo May (1969b, p. 80), one of the most penetrating observers of human experience, speaks of intentionality in this way:

> By this term [intentionality] I do not mean mere intentions, or voluntarism, or purposiveness. I refer to the level of human

experience which underlies them, namely man's capacity to have intentions. Intentionality is the structure which gives meaning to experience. It is our imaginative participation in the coming day's possibilities, out of which participation comes the awareness of our capacity to form, to mold, to change ourselves and the day in relation to each other. This is intentionality.

Intentionality, May goes on to point out, functions both at the conscious and the unconscious levels. "Intentionality is a turning of one's attention toward something; it makes perception possible" (*ibid*, p. 85; see also May, 1969a, pp. 221–245).

The Basic Skill of Inward Searching

One of the most important things my clients have taught me in the thousands of hours we have spent together is how limited we all are in the realization of the potentials we have for depth and breadth of living. Again and again I am astonished to recognize how people who have clearly demonstrated their effectiveness in the external world still live in cramped fashion within their own souls and still have such anguish and frustration in trying to explore within their own lives. And how eagerly they press back limits formerly taken for granted once they learn to trust and use more fully the possibilities lying dormant within them.

In what I am about to write, I want to set forth the present state of my learning about a skill which is as natural to being human as are speech, walking, singing, and many others that we take for granted. Each of these is the development of a potentiality native to the human endowment, a development which can gain immeasurably from learning and practice, a skill which when developed yields increases of satisfaction and effectiveness. I am convinced that we humans have far too little recognized and valued this skill and what it can give us. Many of us are quite primitive in our ability to use it, and some even deny that it exists.

I am talking about a "skill," but in some ways it might better be called an *attitude* or even a kind of mood. What I want to describe is a way of being in our own centers in which we are open to inward awareness so that we can explore within our consciousness, discover fresh conceptions, evolve different ways of seeing familiar circumstances, and extend the range of our personal possibilities. This is a fundamental skill-attitude which the client in intensive psychotherapy needs to develop, but it is much more than that. It is basic to effective and full living. Its significance and use go far beyond the therapy situation. For that reason, I will present what I have learned about it in such a way that the reader, so choosing, may put it to work in daily life. But having said that, let me say promptly that these gains are only to be won by determined follow-through. The reader who would add to present effectiveness in inner searching—and we all have some measure of competence in this—will need to do much more than read to make that gain.

Getting Present

The therapeutic hour is protected from the intrusions we take for granted in so many other life situations. Both participants know that for a fixed amount of time—45, 50, 60 minutes or whatever has been agreed upon—the client's needs are to have priority. That is, in itself, an unusual experience for most people. It sets the stage for more than usual focusing on consciousness. This effect is furthered as usual small talk is reduced in favor of a businesslike concentration on the work at hand, the client's self-exploration. The client comes to appreciate the value of beginning a working period with a time for getting present.

To be truly present is to let go of external matters, to sink down into a feeling of organismic wholeness, to adopt an orientation of awareness in which one's point of consciousness becomes more inward. Getting present is a cumulative process. At first one finds many distracting concerns—the room temperature, an itchy nose, a forgotten phone call, and so on. Gently one disengages from these, only to find a host of distracting inner imps springing into the breach: "I hope I don't get confused like I did last time. . . Ugh! that horrid thought; I don't want to get into *that* now. . . I'll never get settled down. . . What will the doctor think of me. . . Haven't I delayed too long already?" Again it is important to disengage these grasping hands, and to do it gently.

The word *gently* is important to heed. To allow oneself to be caught into fighting against distractions is to be distracted even more. Those who practice meditation know how futile it is to require perfect presence. That is a state infrequently and briefly attained by most of us. What the client needs is to seek more-than-usual wholeness and immediacy of presence, gradually making gains, but expecting no early or total release from distraction.

Adopting a receptive set

Being as present as possible and in a setting dedicated to making one's life better tends spontaneously to bring to the fore one's current life concerns. Even so, it is important to make certain that the concerns are indeed presently alive in consciousness and not simply brought along on a therapy shopping list. The point here is that there will be a crucial difference between the results of engaging in inward search about some matter on which the motivation is an intellectualized feeling, "I *should* work on that" and what the yield will be if the client is impelled by an active and immediate involvement with the same matter. Questions such as the following have the flavor to be desired: "How is my life going these days?. . . Am I having the life I deeply intend for myself?. . . How do I feel right now about being alive?"

Bringing a Concern into Focus

As a sense of concern emerges into awareness, the client needs to be aided in developing it while maintaining presence. This will usually mean that the client comes to value knowing that this concern is uniquely personal just as is the process of exploring it. Both partners must know the therapist will respect the client's priority and sovereignty, indeed will insist upon them. This knowledge can reduce the client's tendency to objectify and manipulate the concern. It is also helpful to realize that what the client is doing in being aware of the concern and seeking to enlarge that awareness is the most constructive thing that can be done by anyone.

I'm trying to convey here an appreciation that is difficult to grasp. The power of human consciousness is great indeed, but it can be made totally ineffectual by objectifying a life concern as though it were an arithmetic problem or an intellectual puzzle. If the client, beginning to be aware of a genuine life concern (e.g., sexual impulses that disrupt life, inability to choose between two courses of action, recurrent periods of depression and futility), makes a problem to be solved of that concern, then the client loses access to the truly creative depths of consciousness. No longer in the privileged and powerful position of being in the center of one's own life, the hope of inward vision enlightening the concern is lost. Instead, the client is no better off than an outside observer trying to puzzle out the solution to the difficulties.

Thus, when awareness of a life concern emerges, the client's intention needs to be to allow it to come to the forefront of awareness, there to be seen as fully as possible but without manipulation or contrivance. An attitude of curiosity, interest, fascination, caring, freed of the urgency to "do something" is what is most to be desired. Other terms that will suggest this approach are *discover*, *appreciate*, and *recognize*.

When the client can do so without disrupting subjective and centered attention to the concern, the next step is to begin describing it to the therapist. However, it is crucial that the report be secondary to the attention on the concern itself, as when one—still half asleep—describes a dream to a companion with the primary centering still being on retaining the images and emotions of the dream rather than on the process of telling it or on the companion's response.

Immersion and Exploration

Everything I've said to this point is preparation for this phase of the process in which the actual exploring within is carried on and in which the creative and healing powers of the person are brought into play. This work begins with the client expressing the concern as fully and subjectively as possible, as I have just described. Doing so and being as open as possible to all inner promptings, one finds that other thoughts, memories, feelings, bodily sensations, and similar inner materials will come to the surface. The client is to mention these in passing, while keeping primary focus on the concern.

As the first telling is completed, the client may find the sense of concern directing attention to one of the associations turned up in the telling. In that case, the client is encouraged to trust that lead and follow the concern. In doing so the set is always to be that of describing internal experience and not sliding off into problem-solving or clue-collecting. It is essential to the task, that the client keep subjectively centered as much as may be possible.

At some point, the client is likely to find the chain of associations running out. This may occur as soon as the first telling is completed, when no sense of concern leads forward; it may be after some time spent in exploring various other awarenesses. When this pause comes, the client is invited to tell the original concern again with the same attitudes of presence and receptivity suggested for the first telling, however, the intent now is different. Rather than simply retelling the original concern as it was then experienced, the client needs to tell it as it is now perceived in light of the materials turned up by the intervening search.

The idea of retelling a concern that one has just finished describing may seem, when viewed from an objective stance, pointless or likely to produce little of value. Actually, quite to the contrary, the retelling is very often extremely productive. For one thing, alert observation will disclose that a person who is truly subjectively centered never—and here I mean *never*—describes a genuine life concern with true subjective centering in the same way twice. I believe that would be literally impossible. The very process of telling about the concern has begun a change process so that subtly, or more obviously, that concern is not experienced quite the same.

Telling and retelling a concern in the manner I am describing deepens one's awareness of it and of what is associated with it in one's depths. It continually broadens and deepens awareness, while usually increasing the emotional involvement in such a way that motivation for change is mobilized.

This is the amazing and all too often unrecognized truth about the human consciousness. It is never a passive recording (such as is made by a camera or tape recorder). It is always a dynamic and creative process, and it is the more so, the more the person having the concern is able to keep truly centered and subjective in the telling of it.

The expectation of discovery

As the client gains some experience with the inward searching process, an important supplementary force comes into being. This force is an expectation of discovery, an attitude which heightens the client's readiness to be open to the unexpected, the changing, and the creative which are awaiting the inward vision. Oftentimes, as this expectation grows, client and therapist realize a growing sense of anticipation, hope, and companionship.

Dealing with Resistances

It is inevitable and appropriate that this process soon encounters resistances. If there were no threats, no old pain, no conflicts in the area of the concern, it would be fully open to awareness in the first place and would not be a focus for this search process. The process is working well when the resistances are brought forward by it.

I sometimes use an analogy to illustrate this important point for my clients. When you are a traveler on a freeway or turnpike and you come to a barricade which forces you to leave the throughway, you are disappointed and inconvenienced. But when you are working on the road crew and you come to that same barricade, you say, "Aha, this is what I'm looking for." So it is in therapy. We're looking for what interferes with the free flow of awareness of the full creative potential of consciousness.

When resistances are encountered, they may take any form whatsoever. Becoming objective about the concern and setting about trying to solve it is a frequent resistance. Getting lost in providing supporting information; switching attention to making certain that the therapist understands all that is involved; becoming critical, belittling, sarcastic, distant, or in some other fashion standing apart from the matter—all of these are resistances often displayed. Trying to do a good job of remaining centered and subjective, checking on the accuracy of the account being given, asking reassurance that the point at issue is not beyond remedy or is not upsetting to the therapist, making comparisons and parallels to other concerns the client has dealt with in the past—these are more subtle (and indeed may not always be resistances but often are).

Almost anything can be used in a resistive fashion; one can never determine from the content. Only the intuition of the therapist can guide him; only the inner vision of the client can firmly determine what is or is not being used resistively. The attempt to keep this judgment objective is itself a resistance to the essentially and absolutely subjective nature of the question. Needless to say, one or both of the participants will frequently mis-estimate what is resistance; that need not be a point on which to get further afield. Perfect accuracy of judgment is neither possible nor necessary.

When resistances are encountered, the client's need is to take note of them gently and then let go of them so far as possible. No effort need be expended in trying to remember or analyze them. If the resistance is truly important, it will recur sufficiently that it can be analyzed in the very process of taking-note-and-relinquishing; further work on it at the moment is apt to become simply a further resistance.

Always the touchstone is centered and subjective awareness with a set to discover and to describe as fully as possible and repeatedly to do just that much and only that much.

The Therapist's Facilitating Role

Clearly the process being described is a highly subjective and individual one. The client is the only one who can carry it out, and that autonomy of the client is essential to the process. Nevertheless, there are important contributions which the therapist can make by way of supporting the client's work.

As I've already suggested, one important function of the therapist is that of disclosing the resistances. This needs to be done with great perceptiveness, sensitivity, and skill, as great as can be managed. The therapist must sense the *red thread* (Saul, 1958) of the client's concern as though it were the artery of essential life blood and then delicately distinguish from it the entangling growth of the resistance. The more clearly it can be exposed, the less it is likely to be confused with the concern itself and the more the professional contributes to making it possible for the client to relinquish the resistance.

In this process, the therapist will often find it helpful to support in low-key ways the patient's feeling of emotional concern. Such comments as "You can feel how much that way of being has cost you all your life" or "You have wanted so much to be loved that you often forgot to take care of your own needs" may help the client keep in touch with how much the work really deals with important elements of life itself.

Too active a therapist participation, however, can disrupt the client's immersion in self-exploration. Great sensitivity is required to know how strongly one can press a confrontation with a resistance without switching the client's inner focus from the concern and the resistance to the relation with the therapist. On the other hand, with highly motivated clients who have really learned to engage in inner searching and who are fully convinced that the therapist is their ally rather than their judge, one can be astonishingly direct, forceful, and insistent.

Summary: The Guiding Conditions of Effective Searching

1. The inner sense of concern is the fundamental element in the process. This focusing of concern aligns the search with one's intentionality. At all times the client must be mindful of what genuinely and personally matters about this issue, what makes a difference in one's life. That awareness may drop into the background as some subaspect becomes more central for a time, but it must never be allowed to fall away entirely.

2. At choice points, when several possible pathways open up, only the client's sense of concern can be trusted to point the direction. Even then, the choices will not infrequently be in error, but there is no other guide that has any claim to the same validity as the client's own sensing. And the client needs to know and value that fact.

3. So far as possible the client does well to adopt an attitude of expectancy, of discovering (rather than reporting). If one knows the continual creativity of the human consciousness and if one opens oneself to be surprised, to find oneself saying things not previously thought, to seeing connections not previously realized—if one can have a set of this kind, then the process is most apt to go well indeed.

4. The client must know right to the marrow that this is an undertaking that is only one's own, that only oneself can carry out, and that this is indeed one's truest opportunity to take direction of one's own life. Knowing this, the client will come to value keeping a truly subjective orientation above all else. It is difficult for many people to realize how imperative is this subjective centering and how fragile it can be at times. More than one client has begun to get into such a centered space only to interrupt the immersion to deal with some triviality ("Oh, I forgot to tell you, I can't come at the usual time on Thursday" or "Nellie, whom I just mentioned, was my father's older sister"). Such a maneuver is, of course, born of a resistance, but it occurs also because the client has not sufficiently appreciated the importance of full presence. I sometimes liken such an event to a person who leaves a motion picture in the middle to make a phone call and then is surprised that the story has gone on during the absence.

5. The client must be prepared to follow wherever the sense of concern may lead. Considerations of propriety, politeness, shame,

good taste, inconvenience for others (e.g. in adjoining offices), or anything else short of important and actual damage to some person must all be regarded simply as resistances to the process. Similarily, logical connections, consistency of viewpoint, appropriateness of emotions, and similar aspects are irrelevant to the primary function of ruthless and thorough exploration of the client's concern.

6. Recognition, that one can never do this process perfectly or for as long as one may desire, is necessary if the client is going to persist sufficiently to develop the skill and mine it for all it can yield. No one I know—and I certainly include myself—can readily get into this searching posture, can maintain it as long as seems desirable, can follow the red thread with sureness, or invariably emerge with abundant results. One needs to take it for granted that there will be difficulties, that one will lose the way, and that repeatedly one will have to go back to "go" and begin again. Then, and only then, will the person genuinely have a means for taking charge of her or his own life.

Client Steps in Intensive Psychotherapy

Each client's experience of existential-humanistic psychotherapy is unique, and that is as it should be. However, it is possible to pick out some of the milestones passed by many who travel this way. Not every client notes all of these markers; some seem to touch but few; still there is enough generality to warrant describing them.

The descriptions which follow assume that the major client task of learning to search within in a centered and concerned manner is going forward and that the client is thus moving in a growth-ward direction. These are some of the phases many such clients go through.

Making a Genuine and Major Commitment to Self-exploration

This is, of course, the foundation step. The work of examining one's life and setting about bringing it into greater accord with one's deeper intent is not a casual thing. It cannot be likened to going to a physician to be cured of a disease, consulting a broker to plan one's investment portfolio, or even to attending a college to earn a degree. Each of these actions, as with most of those which make up the usual round of our lives, can be carried out with only limited investment of our own being. Not so with truly intensive psychotherapy; it demands a major investment of our emotional capital.

For this reason, intensive psychotherapy is not something for everyone, by any means. Clients do well to consider carefully before undertaking such a course. It is usually one of the two or three most significant ventures of a lifetime, and it is often one of the major financial outlays as well. Because of the demandingness of this conception, people who choose psychotherapy tend to be from a restricted segment of the social-economic scale (although not exclusively so) characterized by higher than usual level of education and income. Their motivations frequently are derived from having tried but been dissatisfied with less thoroughgoing therapy or from professional reasons for seeking a comprehensive degree of self-understanding. There are also those who come to this therapy only casually understanding what is involved but then find it so congenial and so exciting that they are drawn forward toward full investment.

> Weighing whether to undertake so total a psychotherapy can be a conflictful experience. "Have I the right to spend so much time and money on myself? Does it mean that something is very seriously wrong with me? I'm fascinated by what this experience might mean in my life, but I'm afraid of it too. I've always felt that there is so much more that I could have in life, if only I could use my own powers better. Can I really trust the therapist so much? I'd really like finally to come to terms with all the confusion and mixed up things inside of me."

Developing an Accepting Attitude Toward Oneself

In learning the inward searching process, one must adopt an attitude of openness toward what one finds within. Those who have, as do so many of us, lifelong habits of treating themselves as objects to be figured out or as troublesome subordinates to be criticized and corrected, continually disrupt their own efforts to be open. Gradually they can learn to listen to their own feelings and impulses with acceptance which is not approval but which expresses a determination to have genuine self-understanding. This is the step which most makes possible desired changes, in marked contrast to the difficulty in growing typical of those who feel compelled to pass judgment on each attitude, emotion, or impulse that they uncover.

> How much can one accept and still live with oneself? Must one truly be open to everything? If I let it all out, won't it mean that I'll never change? It's all well and good to say that one must accept before being able to change what is inside, but that's for ordinary people. But what a relief to quit fighting myself all the time! I've fought some of these battles as long as I can remember, and it hasn't done much damn good, so far as I can see.

Lessening Concern with Usual Social Controls

Much of the business of childhood, for many of us, centered around learning the "right" ways of being, doing, thinking, speaking, and relating to the world around us. Parents, often implicitly, have seen their task that of domesticating the wild animal into an acceptable child. To many in the middle-class culture, being proper, being rational, being moderate, and being pleasing became the new commandments. Seldom was *be yourself* meant except as an injunction to avoid excess or silliness or assuming too much positively about oneself. Our own impulses had to thread a mine field of prohibitions and admonitions and usually emerged into action as crippled residues of the original vital strivings.

Intensive psychotherapy offers the client a cultural island cut off from the mainland of usual social niceties. It is a refuge in which the client can be naked in the sunlight of one's own awareness, can stretch and run and shout unrestrainedly. It's a place and time in which there is a setting aside of most limits, except those necessary to protect client, therapist, and others from lasting hurt. The commitment to inward exploration and to growth is given priority over most of the restraints familiar in daily life. My injunction to clients is often, "Think anything, feel anything, say anything, and then *choose* what you will do." The message is that one needs to be free within one's own consciousness; only at the level of actions is there apt to be important consequences which the client must weigh.

> But you can't really mean "anything"—say anything? I learned a long time ago to watch myself carefully or I'd do things that. . . But then you said choose my *actions;* so otherwise I can

be free. I see. That makes it easier. Let me tell you about. . . Oh, oh, it's not so easy to say it either. Well, I'll try. Maybe I could really let it all come out. What a thought! And why stop with saying it. I'd really like to let go all the way for once, but. . . .

Limits

What are the limits of acceptable actions in psychotherapy? There is much debate on this question these days. Must the client be confined solely to verbal exploration; if not, how much action may be permitted or encouraged? Therapists are experimenting with these questions (Bugental, 1968; 1976, p. 314). Some see an erosion of professional responsibility occurring; others insist it is an extension of that obligation. As usual, the argument is most bitter around sexual and aggressive impulses. I don't know any fully satisfactory solution. Traditional limits are certainly too confining and even anti-therapeutic at times; but there are real dangers in releasing impulses long stored and much conflicted. Only courage, open-mindedness, and increased communication can bring us toward some resolution.

Discovering an Enlarged Sense of Possibility for Oneself

One of the more profound recognitions that comes with the development of the skill of genuine inner searching is the realization of how arbitrary is the particular pattern of one's life and how chance-dictated is one's history. So easily might things have worked out differently, so readily might other choices have been taken, other relationships developed, other opportunities acted upon. How differently things might have worked out *if only* a small change had occurred at any of a dozen different junctures. This can be a fascinating, an exciting discovery; it can also be terrifying, seeming to take the solid ground from under one's feet. The client experiences as actual that there are indeed an infinity of ways one might be; that the limited range known in the past is not an unchangeable set of tracks along which one must run out the rest of life. Instead, the client realizes, one has the freedom—and the responsibility, like it or not—of creating one's self again and again. Yet each day is irrevocably as it is, and freedom always lies in the new moment.

So I can see that I might have become a scientist instead of a salesman, big deal! I could have married Joan instead of Lois;

I've always known that. I could have been the president of the company and flown like a bird too; so what else is new? President of the company? Come on . . . but just think about it. Hey, you know, it really is so? That's an amazing idea when you really stop to think about it. If I'd taken that training when I had the chance and played my cards a little smarter with Old Alec. . . I kind of knew that at the time, you know, but hell I was so mad at him that I got more fun out of putting him down. Not so smart, not so smart, and that's a fact. And that's not the first time I've had to show somebody up and ended up behind the eight ball myself. Who needs that? I sure don't. President of the company . . . hmmm. . . Hell! what a ridiculous daydream that is. Or is it? I'm not over the hill yet . . . .

Renewing Determination to See the Job Through

One of the essential ingredients in this whole enterprise, and one too easily taken for granted, is the sheer courage and determination of the person who hangs in through all the pain, the discouragement, the short-lived successes; the desert dry times of no evident gain; the terror or archaic fears suddenly alive and very real; and the omnipresent realization that there is no possible guarantee of a happy ending. To be sure, a very high percentage of clients who genuinely get involved in this process see it through, but it is a testimony to the resilience of the human spirit that this is so.

As therapy begins, the client nearly always believes that it won't take nearly as long as the therapist suggests (usually two to three years). This attitude is not due to vanity; it is rather born of too little appreciation of the astounding breadth and depth one is about to enter. So few of us really are aware of the immense universe within, of the many possibilities, the multiple interweavings of feelings, imaginings, hopes, fears, impulses, strivings, memories, ponderings, and all else that fills that unique middle earth within which each of us, knowingly or not, dwells.

We are blocked from knowing that immensity by the walls which we have erected to hold back what is frightening, guilty, or painful. Dismantling those walls results in releasing the very feelings which in the past we deemed too distressing to be borne. Yet it is only through experiencing those dreaded hurts and seeing them through that we can come to terms with our own being, discover our native freedom, and enter into the vastness within. This is a process which calls for all of our determination and trust—trust in ourselves, in the therapist, and in the process itself.

Enlarging One's Sense of Identity

Who or what are we humans? What is our deeper nature? What is possible for us? What degree of governance of our own destinies can we assert? What powers have we when we are at our fullest? What is it like to be wholly at one with ourselves, no longer divided within? These are the questions which implicitly and explicitly are explored by the client and therapist as their work advances. The usual outcome of solid therapeutic exploration of one's being is a greatly enlarged intuition of that being, of one's power to have life experiences closer to one's deep wanting, and of one's essential trustworthiness when not alienated from self.

Keeping faith with oneself

Essential to this enlarged being is the client's coming to value keeping faith with oneself. We learned to double-cross ourselves so readily. For example, a client feels sad over the loss of a valued relationship, and then abruptly adopts a harsh tone, saying "Always mooning over spilt milk; what a crybaby!" Another shares an aspiration to write a great book, then switches to self-mocking, "That'll be the day! I ought to come down out of the clouds and get something done in the real world rather than daydreaming all the time." A third client can only describe her yearning to be a mother in a sarcastic voice, and a fourth reveals his misery over his rift with his son only between the lines of his self-blaming tirade. None of these people is keeping faith. Hardly any of them would think of treating another person in the same way they are treating themselves, but the attitude seems to be, "It doesn't matter if I'm unkind to myself; after all I probably deserve it, and it's certainly better than being too soft with myself."

> You say I need to keep faith with myself, but you don't know what a mess I am inside. My only hope is to whip myself into better shape, then I might risk being at one with myself. I want to be the sort of person I could be and not settle for this incomplete, weak, dishonest self. Yet I can feel how much I give up

> hope when I turn on myself that way. Standing away from myself, I'm saying to you, "I know you must despise someone like that, and I do too. So don't judge me by the way I am but by the way I look down on that way of being just as you do. . . Only maybe you don't."

As we begin to experience our own determination to accept whatever we find within our own being, we take back into ourselves the center of gravity which we had given over to the imagined judgment of others or to society or to some institution (e.g., the church). We claim our birthright, our own sovereignty in our own lives, and we relinquish the cop-out of blaming influences (persons, circumstances, institutions) outside of ourselves. From this we gain a sense of largeness within ourselves, a developing feeling of personal dignity.

Broadening the range of subjective experiencing

When the client begins to take a stance of genuinely accepting all that is found in awareness, of continuing the search wherever it will lead, and of keeping faith with oneself in an enlarged sense of identity, then the client will begin to discover how much of subjective experiencing has previously been denied and how much that denial has kept one from realizing what is potential. Customarily we treat experiences of incompleteness, ambiguity, and conflict, sad and angry feelings, times of grief and guilt as unwelcome intrusions to be rid of as soon as possible. All of these are inescapably part of every human being's experience; each has important contributions to make to the wholeness and depth of experience. We rid ourselves of them at great cost to our humanness.

> I know I need to get into those feelings about my father and his death, and I guess I'll be glad when I'm through them; but boy, do I dread what all that is going to stir up inside of me. I mean, Dad was a wonderful guy and all, but he could also be a real bastard at times. What comes to mind now is the time when he was drunk and. . . And I felt so sorry for him and so mad at him at the same time. God! I didn't know I had so much pain and so many tears still stored up inside me. . . I know that I'm like him in a lot of ways. Sometimes that makes me sad—or even angry. But other times, I'm glad, and even kind of proud. . . . You know it's been several months since I worked on my feelings

about Dad, and I just realized that when I think of him now I have a kind of good feeling, but I know he's really gone now, and that's sad.

The emotions and conflicts within us which once we sought only to be rid of are usually but the surfaces of whole areas of inner experiencing which have the potential for enriching and illuminating our lives. This doesn't mean that we need welcome those uncomfortable and painful times. They're going to come along in any event. But when we experience such turmoil and discomfort, we will be better able to do something about them if our approach is that of exploration rather than simply that of trying to flush them as quickly as possible.

Committing to Life-long Growth

Eventually the experience of self-exploration, continued over some time and carried into all aspects of one's life, leads to the client's recognition that the job will never be completed. Many people enter psychotherapy with the same attitude that they have when taking their car to be repaired: "Let's get it fixed so we can get it back on the road. It's no good to me in the garage." This model is consistent with the older doctor-patient view of psychotherapy; the physician should set the broken arm or prescribe for the infection so that the patient can get back to normal health. Existential-humanistic psychotherapy may certainly serve this function, but it opens up possibilities that extend far beyond simple repair or restoration of health. In time the client comes to recognize that growth through the skill of inward searching is central to a full life and can—indeed, desirably will—continue throughout life.

This recognition often comes as a prelude to the client's getting ready to discontinue the formal therapeutic relationship. As the client realizes that the task will never be completed, that it is a continuing and enriching part of life, there is likely to be the recognition also that one can now go on without the support and facilitation of the therapist.

I've been wondering lately if we shouldn't cut down the frequency with which I'm coming in. It seems to me that our work still needs to go on, but I find I get a lot of it done when I'm not here, like when I'm driving along alone I do a lot of thinking, or sometimes after the family's in bed. . . Here's my statement and my check. You know, for the first time in quite a while, when I made out that check I thought, "Wow, that's a lot of money; I sure could use it in other ways these days."

A frequent mark of a successful course of intensive psychotherapy is the continued growth which the client carries into effect *after* leaving therapy. Again and again I've noted that clients seem to make some of their most profound gains in the first year or two after termination. It seems likely that discontinuing the work with the therapist brings home as nothing else could the fact that the choices and the responsibility are really the client's. If things are to be different, then one must make them different.

A Client's Account of Working in Therapy

As I became accustomed to being in therapy, most of the initial fear dropped away, except usually at the beginning of each session I felt anxiety. This seemed to be related to fear of the unknown—of what we would discover. The anxiety usually was gone once we started to work. I came to really look forward to my sessions. In fact, it became the most central and important thing in my life. I was learning new aspects of myself that were really old parts that I had lost connection and identity with. I found that Jim trusted me no matter what I expressed or was. I kept waiting for the axe to fall, waiting for his disapproval, his rejection, but it never came. As time went along this acceptance of me had a profound effect on me. I began to develop a deep trust in my own experience of life—*in my own reality*. . . . He continually said by his behavior, in words, action and feeling that he trusted me; trusted my process, trusted my ability to sense what felt right for me, trusted my sense of reality. He encouraged me to pay attention to the deeper aspects of my own being and to discern the difference between programs or should-statements that were learned from the outside and internal processes of my own genuine feeling and sense of things. I can't in words share how terribly important and central this learning to trust myself has been for me. It is the most fundamentally important thing that has happened to me in my whole life. By

> developing this self-trust, it was like a runaway train being placed on its *own* track. I discovered that there was an internal me—an internal process, a living—that was continually alive, changing, unfolding, directing, moving, being. I also discovered that this internal central being was much more me, much more genuine than any of my external behaviors, and yet this internal me was much more, *ever so much more than just the me that I had always thought I was.* This paradox was and is the most central thing in my life and has directed my life ever since. If I hadn't been put on my own track by the trust Jim gave me, this great event couldn't have happened to me. The great event that I'm referring to came late in the therapy process.
>
> I had become fully accustomed to coming, lying down on the couch, being quiet, waiting and listening with my inner ear and eye to the process of life that was happening in me at that moment. As always, after some indefinite period of time—anywhere from several minutes to about 15 minutes—something began to appear in the window of my inner eye—my awareness. In this particular instance what appeared was a very intense uneasiness. I stayed with it and went with it like a cowboy breaking a bronco. This was no easy task, but with Jim's continual help, direction, and support, I had learned to be aware of and resist the attempts of my personal life or my personality to move away from the center of activity when there was unrest. I learned that I could move so far away by various means, such as thinking critically about myself, going to sleep, paying attention to external sounds and sights, etc., that I lost all sense of being present. In this instance, as I tuned into the uneasiness, it built and built until it was almost a panic. As I struggled to stay with it and not run away, its essence began to become clear to my consciousness. It became apparent to me that I was afraid of not existing (Cogswell, 1977).

What followed (not to keep the reader in suspense) was a transcendent experience of a kind which comes to some clients in the latter stages of intensive psychotherapy. This is appropriately part of our discussion of therapeutic outcomes in Chapter 8. What is significant at this point is the demonstration of how the search process may reach into realms of experience beyond our familiar world (see also Bugental, 1976, Chapter 8).

7

Each Journey is New for the Guide as well as the Traveler: The Chief Aspects of the Psychotherapist's Contribution

And so the travelers progress; subtly they become companions; each changes, and each changes the other as the journey alters both. No amount of experience can ready the guide for all contingencies, nor can safe passage be ensured for client or guide. The events of the trip must be met as they arise, and both venturers have their parts in how they are met and how the destination is approached.

We turn now to the psychotherapist's work. What are the main contributions that the professional can make to the success of the client's therapeutic endeavor? (It should be clear by now that ultimately this enterprise is the client's and not the therapist's.) The therapist can never fulfill the task by participating in a standardized way; no amount of training in or loyalty to any system of psychotherapy can take the place of the human presence and potentiality of infinite adaptability of the person who is the therapist.

Five hundred years before the birth of Christ, Heraclitus said, "It is not possible to step twice into the same river." Nor can the psychotherapist conduct any two sessions—let alone any two psychotherapies—in the same way. For this reason, it will be more valid for me to write in the first person in this chapter particularly.

The Working Therapeutic Alliance

Joining in Developing a Unique Relationship

Each client who comes to psychotherapy brings a unique constellation of needs, expectancies, apprehensions, emotional patterns, and readiness to make a constructive relationship. The complexity, subtlety, and variety of such constellations is such that any attempt to objectify them is foredoomed. Instead, only the most subtle and comprehensive of all instruments—an aware human receptivity—must be relied on to discover how this particular matching of therapist and client may most promisingly be brought into being.

I have learned to proceed slowly, waiting to grasp my client's perspective, sensing the timing of questions and information-giving which will be most apt to result in clear communication and reinforce the consciousness that this is an important life decision. The first priority must be given (if not the first place in sequence) to ensuring that the client has a real opportunity to say that which presses for expression: pain or fear, hopes and misgivings, the need to assert businesslike control (see Chapter 2). Equally important is giving the client some chance to experience what I am like. This does not mean that I need to engage in extensive self-disclosure, giving information about myself. It does mean that I will say something of how I work and what I expect from the client.

Teaching the search process

In the last chapter I described at some length the fundamental human skill of inward searching. Each of us has some degree of experience in using this talent already, but often our way of using it is complicated or interfered with by prejudices and erroneous information ("You have to concentrate very hard to get fresh ideas," or "Just imagining things is a waste of time," or "The sooner you get over feeling bad about something the better," or "You mustn't pay too much attention to your wanting because it will get you dissatisfied with your life"). Discerning the often subtle influence of such attitudes, the therapist seeks to expose their operations and their destructive consequences. Concurrently, the therapist watches for and lends reinforcement to the healthful attitudes and skills the client already possesses. This is a demanding and fundamentally important part of the therapist's mission.

Monitoring the Relationship

It's hard to overestimate the importance of the therapist keeping aware of how the relationship with the client is going. This is not to say that that relation needs always to be smooth and untroubled. Some very productive times are triggered by misunderstandings, disagreements, fights, and even antagonisms. The quality the relation needs to have as much as possible is authenticity. It must be a genuine relationship between the two human beings involved, and it must provide an emotional setting in which both seek to be as genuine as possible. The manner of the client's being authentic in the relation is different from the therapist's way, but it is essential that both seek toward being real with each other.

To be authentic in the relation, my client needs to bring all needs and hopes and fears into the therapeutic hour itself. One cannot come solely to report on experiences one has at other times. The client must risk being present with present emotions, immediate distortions, living strivings, and current flights from life. This sounds and is somewhat paradoxical, and the therapist's task is, in an important degree, to help the client confront this paradox and continue to work toward being as wholly and as nakedly present as possible.

The therapist monitors the client's participation to try to be aware of the ways in which the client is withholding genuine presence, to try to pick up clues to what may be threatening the client in relation to the therapist, and to sense the general degree of distress the client is experiencing in order to modulate therapist activity and to know how much support or structure the client may need at any particular time.

The therapist's feelings

Concurrently, if I am wise, I will monitor my own feelings toward this particular client and toward the way our work together is progressing. Often my feelings—such as, sleepiness, sexual arousal, annoyance, unusual bursts of caring—will be important clues to things within myself which may intrude inappropriately or to client efforts to manipulate me in some way. In either case, early and full therapist awareness is most desirable.

An underlying bond

Under everything else in our relationship, I seek and count on an understanding that is rarely expressed in words. This is our mutual knowing that I am on the side of the client having more life, of the client's push toward less troubled and richer living; in short, of the client's hope. If, after we have worked together for a time, either of us doesn't know that, somehow we don't go on together. Something happens. The client loses motivation and withdraws, or I don't encourage continuing once the first relief from symptoms has occurred.

From my side, my unspoken contract with the client's hope is that I will stand by that hope to the best of my ability, no matter what the client may need to get into. And sometimes the client needs to make some pretty rough tests of that dedication: I have known bitter personal attacks, accusations of being only concerned with money or with getting material for writing, verbal attacks on my family, threats to my name and reputation, refusals to pay overdue fees, suicide threats, and much else. Generally, I've been able to stand pretty firm because under all this I still could sense the person there, secretly extending a hand and begging not to be deserted. A few times I've missed, and for most of them, the clients in such instances came through for me, hanging in largely on the basis of what we had had together the rest of the time. It can be a very tough business for one or both of us at times, and it can take forms that aren't what most textbooks describe (e.g., being hit by a client and hitting back, locking the door and refusing to let a client leave until she changed an avowed intention to suicide).

Attending Seriously to the Client's Work

The great bulk of my attention to work during the hour is directed to the processes of the client's activity rather than to the content. I am concerned to assess the degree to which my partner is genuinely present—accessible to the inner stream of awareness and expressive of all that is found there. I am continually alert to pick up clues to any reduction of subjective centering, to the tendency to stand apart from oneself in judgment or shame or some other way. I listen for the subtle changes in voice or manner which tell of conflicting impulses or of a detour around a threatening area.

This may all sound as though my conception of my work as a therapist is that of policing the way the client talks to me. Nothing could be farther from the case, although at times a client experiences me as a kind of nagging parent or therapeutic conscience. That is itself a resistance to be disclosed and worked through. My function is that of being my client's ally, of supporting the client's effort to be authentically present and effectively self-exploring. I am not trying to "catch" failures at being so. I know all too well—from listening to so many people and from my own inner searching—how difficult it is to do this work. As an ally, I can take some of the load, freeing the client to immerse in what is being disclosed by the searching.

Most clients come, in time, to value this supporting function of my noting and calling their attention to the ways they are pushed around by their fears, guilts, shames, and conflicts. The rewards of recognizing these are so direct in freeing energies and in feelings of greater choice and sureness in knowing one's own inner wants and fears that the client soon welcomes whatever will aid in increasing awareness.

Locus of concern

One of the distinguishing characteristics of the kind of therapy I'm describing is *where* the attention of the client is directed. Look at these examples:

CL–1: I keep losing my train of thought because I'm wondering what you think of all this stuff I've been telling you.
TH–1A: What do you imagine that I think about it?
TH–1B: Even when I'm not saying anything you keep wondering about me, eh?

TH–1C: It's hard for you to keep with your own flow when someone else hears what's going on in you.

Now look at each of the therapist responses in terms of where the client is directed to focus concern. In TH–1A, the attention is in the direction of the therapist (the fact that it concerns the patient's imagining or projection is secondary). In TH–1B, the focus is on the relation between therapist and client; while in TH–1C, the locus of concern is within the client's own effort to search inwardly. Of course, there is something of each participant in each response —inevitably in view of what the client has just said—but it is the relative emphasis that I'm talking about here.

Many therapies operate chiefly in the direction of the therapist; this is especially characteristic of some of the action-oriented approaches, such as Gestalt, bioenergetics, and psychodrama. Others tend to cluster around the relation or transaction between the partners—this is true of some of the ego-analytic approaches and of relationship approaches of humanistic counseling. For the kind of work I am concerned with, the primary locus must be within the client's own experiencing for the bulk of our time.

Having just said that, let me hasten to add that there are important periods during which the relationship is the appropriate locus and others—though less frequent—where the therapist is. Both of these times tend in my work to come after the client has gained a strong hold on the skill of inward searching. I say "tend to come" because there are exceptions, when concern about me or about our relation defeats the client's efforts to work on the inner flow of awareness, and so we must deal with these intrusions before anything else.

Reflecting on client's experience

So many of the people whom I see have learned to treat themselves as objects—and, at that, objects to which they have only mild attachment. They hurry past their inner experiencing in an effort to report fully and accurately on these objects, and they regard my attention to the subjective as quaint, kindly, and impractical.

CL–2: I tried every way I could think of to persuade her not to go, but I just couldn't get through to her. I wonder if I'd gotten her sister to. . . .

TH–2: You really wanted to reach her, somehow, some way.

CL-3 Huh? Oh, yeah, I sure did. But anyway, I got to wondering if maybe her sister might have been able to. . . .
TH-3: It seems to surprise you that I reflect on how much you wanted to get through to her.
CL-4 Oh, no, that's all right. It's just that I was thinking about whether someone else. . . .
TH-4: Your own feelings seem beside the point of how you might have handled things better.
CL-5: Well, yes, I guess so. I never thought about it that way.

It is important to the development of true inner awareness and to one's coming home to one's own life for the client to be attuned to inward emotional responses to experiences. Nearly every therapeutic approach makes much use of the question, "What are you feeling?" or "How do you feel about that?" or "What does that feel like?" This is so frequent because of the endemic affect-blindness of our time. Yet those questions generally leave me dissatisfied when I'm trying to help a client get with the inner flow. Phrased as I've just illustrated, the questions seem to me to evoke the client's somewhat self-conscious *idea of what she or he might be feeling* as often as the actual but unrecognized feelings. Long clinical experience —not mine alone but that of many others—has demonstrated that it is often more effective to direct attention to the resistance rather than what it resists. Accordingly, I try to point out how the client slights or overlooks emotions rather than asking that they be named directly.

What the Therapist Does

Intervening in the Flow of the Client's Awareness

An idealized picture of the therapeutic process would be something like this:

Henry enters and after an exchange of greetings gets settled in the chair or on the couch. He is silent several minutes as he gets deeply centered in his innerness; then he begins relating what he finds there, following its turnings and twistings, expressing emotions that arise, discovering connections, realizing applications to his daily life. Occasionally I underscore a feeling, comment on a hesitation, or point to a brief loss of immersion, but for the most part the client is self-maintaining.

While this is an extreme sketch, it serves as a useful guide to therapist activity. My role is chiefly that of helping the client approximate this model as much as possible. Therefore the less I intrude on the flow of associations, the better. On the other hand, at times I must be quite intrusive, interrupting the substitutes for authentic inner searching.

Use of the couch

The couch is often associated with blank-screen psychoanalytic detachment. It need not be tied to that mode, however. I have a couch available in my office, and in each client's therapy, I introduce the couch and suggest getting familiar with its aid. Thereafter, for the most part it is the client who chooses whether or not to lie down. Most of my clients who work intensively with good inward searching skill find the couch frequently helpful during the long central portion of their work. The reclining position has associations of inwardness, reverie, detachment from daily routine, and life review—all of which are appropriate to the task at hand.

Low therapist profile

Although I have personally become much more active in my work than I once thought desirable (Bugental, 1965, p. 115), I still believe that the therapist does well to talk much less than the client for the most part. Too much therapist talk prevents the client's deeply immersing in the flow of inner awareness. Thus a tendency to talk *about* oneself rather than *out of* oneself is fostered. This is a difference that really makes a difference. Contrast these two client statements:

CL–6A: I feel strongly that I don't want to be like my father in the way I am with my family. He was so autocratic and domineering. I am determined that I want my children to know they can say anything to me, and I'll try to give them a full hearing.

CL–6B: So there I was rushing to get to the meeting on time—I mean, you can imagine, with all those people counting on me. Anyway there I was gulping down a cup of coffee and putting on my coat at the same time and

> wouldn't you know Sally would pick right that minute to have the hysterics about some fool thing at school! I mean, I'm trying to do the best I can for everybody, and she hasn't the common decency to let the thing wait till I get home. No, she has to have an answer right now! Well, I gave her an answer all right! I guess she'll be a little more aware of other people next time and not just think of herself always. I don't know, I just can't see what gets into kids. . .

This man is not hypocritical and is not unfeeling; he is very human. We all have two sets of attitudes and perceptions. One is at the level of conscious perception of ourselves and circumstances. This level is a valid one, and it is this level from which we guide many of our choices. But there is another level, which is that of implicit and unreflective action. At this level we respond more frequently on the basis of unrecognized patterns stemming from earlier years and especially from experiences of strong emotional impact. The conflicts between the two are often unrecognized but very frequently are the sources of distress and self-rejection. Much of the work of therapy is concerned with bringing from the subconscious the patterns of this second level of perception, so that it may be put beside the patterns of the first level and the client can bring about more coherence within.

So it is that I am concerned with helping my client to become immersed in genuine inner searching, which then opens up the level of implicit perception and helps the client get to the "controls" of much that he or she experiences and does. Lacking that perception, the client has previously regarded feelings and actions as without reason or at odds with her or his own values. Too much activity on my part keeps the client at the more conscious self-perception level.

Keeping a low therapist profile at first, and to some extent at all times, has the advantage also of demonstrating that this is not a usual, social situation and tends to reduce the client's tendency to use her or his usual social skills as defenses. Finally, relative therapist silence results in greater impact when the therapist does choose to say something.

Of course, this last consideration is an ambivalent one. Sometimes I am glad of that added impact; sometimes I'd like to be free of it. It can be helpful in bringing the attention of the client to something (a resistance pattern, for example) needing awareness, but it can also make such an intrusion out of anything I do that even a casual aside gets blown into sticky immensity.

CL-7: We argued for hours about it. I get so tired of trying to get her to see the point, and I suppose she. . . .
TH-7: (yawning) Oh, sorry, up late last night.
CL-8: Oh, sure. Well, she—I'll bet it's boring to have to sit and listen to drivel like this all day long.
TH-8: No, no. It's quite all right. Please go on.
CL-9: Sure. Well, we argued, like I said, and—Would you like me to open the window? It's kind of stuffy in here.
TH-9: Thanks, no. Why don't you just go on telling me about the argument and how it made you feel?
CL-10: Well, I felt awful about it. I try to be understanding, you know, but—I suppose she gets bored with me too. I know I talk a lot sometimes, and I ought to pay more attention to how other people. . .

Insisting on Client Good Faith

I have already described how important it is to help the client learn to keep faith. The habits of distancing from oneself, of being sarcastic, critical, angry with one's own being are so disfiguring and destructive, yet so widespread. One of the ways I often intervene is to deal with this tendency, for it quite disrupts the client's immersion and leads to a kind of alienated recital, which is largely defeating of genuine self-exploration.

CL-11: I really felt bad about the way I blasted Sally, but. . . . Well, I *say* I felt bad, but I keep blowing up at people, so who's going to believe I feel so all fired bad?
TH-11: Do you?
CL-12: Do I what?
TH-12: Do you believe you feel badly about blowing up at Sally?
CL-13: Sure, I guess so.
TH-13: You don't seem very sure.
CL-14: Well, hell, if you'd said it as many times as I had and then turned right around, and . . .

TH-14: That's another matter. The question was whether you do or do not feel badly about blowing up at Sally, and so far I don't see you taking any time to find out really because you're so busy telling me how inconsistent you are.

CL-15: Well, I think—No, wait a minute, let me feel into that. (Pause, then in a changed and sobered voice.) Hey, you know, I really do feel badly about that. I mean I hardly knew it till just now, and . . .

Leading Toward an Expanded Sense of Identity

Most people operate out of largely unexamined ideas of their own identities. Thus I try to bring my client's own self-conception to consciousness. Similarly, many of my interventions are designed to challenge existing self-pictures and to suggest enlarged awareness of being. When most people enter therapy they regard themselves as chiefly what is conscious or "on file." Implicitly they demonstrate that they also know they are more than that; however, when they come to deal with life issues, they seldom count on or know how to have access to that "more." Repeatedly people say they have exhausted all possibilities on the basis of a most superficial survey within. They act as though the fact that nothing readily comes to mind demonstrates that nothing could under any circumstances. Most people have very few skills which they recognize as available to tap into what is latent within them or to create new approaches or awarenesses. Indeed clients often enter therapy with the conviction that someone else must help them, since they have exhausted everything they can call on within themselves. This is all the more striking when one considers how often the clients entering the kind of therapy I'm describing are people of demonstrated creativity and effectiveness in the outer world. (See the accounts of such therapy in Bugental, 1976.)

It is my purpose, by repeated and varied interventions, to suggest, imply, teach, and call for clients to seek, find, and explore for the "more" which is within them. This is the basic thrust of much that I do. By every means I can muster—of which explicit telling is one of the less important—I put over that the clients are overlooking, ignoring, devaluing something I regard as very important in their capacities. Some of the forms this communication takes include my refusal to accept statements that they have reached a limit:

CL–16: So I'll be damned if I can see why I keep blowing up like that. God knows I don't like doing it. I've thought and thought about it, but I don't come up with anything.
TH–16: It's hard to imagine you don't come up with anything at all.
CL–17: Nothing. Flat out zero.
TH–17: Why don't you try it right now. Think about it out loud and let's see what happens.

And, of course, what happens is that such clients soon reveal that they are disrupting their own inward searching in a variety of ways, and, when they relinquish these interruptions, they begin to get into the roots of such angry outbursts.

Demonstrating the larger identity

Various events in therapy occur spontaneously and evidence the "more," which is latent in all clients. For example, clients successfully explore within, achieving awarenesses which they would not have consciously known to seek out and which, quite obviously, I could not have suggested. Ben began his search with concern about being late for the session, but ultimately arrived at a previously unrecognized anger at his mother. Penny went from sadness over leaving a marriage to intense anxiety about relinquishing the props to her sense of identity. Such instances give me a powerful opportunity to emphasize that there is much more latent in the client.

In this same way, I call clients' attention to how dreams and waking fantasies are expressions of a larger consciousness. So many people are accustomed to dismissing these as unrealistic, impractical, and wasteful, missing their clear significance of our truer and larger nature. Dreams and fantasies are ways of transcending the everyday, preparing the way for creativity, and opening up richer resources for our lives.

Using therapist example

By my example, I teach the larger identity of human beings when I do not try to deal with the content of my client's talk but confine my attention to the process of searching. As I focus on the search-

searching and not what it discloses, I demonstrate the client has a unique position in dealing with life concerns (and that mine is ultimately a secondary role). I point out whenever possible how clients have led us to materials I would not have thought to suggest, but which clearly illuminate their concerns. In doing this I often find I have, and let show, emotional responses such as delight, teariness, or surprise.

Perhaps that is as important as anything I can say in this regard. I feel humble and respectful of the truer nature of human beings. We live so shallowly in contrast to the depths and richness which are constantly revealed to and concealed from me. I want for myself and for those with whom I share so much more experience of being in touch with, living in accord with, and living fully in our truer natures.

Being Present, Caring, and Modeling

One of the most fundamental things I can do for a client is something that is difficult to put into words in such a way as to convey its full significance. The three terms, *being present, caring, and modeling,* do as well as any, but they are only suggestive. I've already described how necessary it is for me to feel a genuine involvement with my client's struggle if I am to be as effective in giving aid as we both wish. This is, by no means, only something "nice" to do or something helpful to our relationship. It is absolutely essential if I am going to be able to tune into the implicit, the deeply subjective, and the nascent in my client. And the way to do that is to be as present and caring for my client's emergence as is genuine. And in being so with the client, I am modeling a way of regarding that person's experience and life which hopefully the client will come in time to share. More than one client has told me, "I could feel your caring so surely that I decided maybe I could care about myself too."

This point of view is at some odds with the ideal of clinical detachment that has been traditional in the healing arts. Perhaps that is just another way in which this approach is at contrast with usual medical models. I think, however, it is more than that. I think the traditional model, which is part and parcel of the whole attitude of estrangement from the subjective life which we have repeatedly recognized in these pages, was born of a mistrust of emotions and of relationships. Our culture has long sensed the immense recesses of the human spirit, which have been little explored, and has reacted to that sensing with anxiety and denial. Like a person who inherits a great house and lives in but a small part of it because the balance, now locked off, is deemed to be ghost-occupied, we have limited ourselves out of superstition. It is my belief that human emotions are to be trusted and that caring is itself a healing influence.

Client needs—therapist needs

What I am saying may easily be misunderstood as advocating confusing my own needs with my client's, and that I do *not* mean. I care about my clients, their experience, their pain, their frustration, and the loss of their lives in self-destructive patterns of living. I care that they suffer. I do not suffer that they suffer. I do not need them to stop suffering so that I will stop vicariously and empathically suffering, for I am not hurting because they hurt. I care about them and their lives, but I do not need them to claim more of those lives in order to validate my life. I rejoice with them when they gain facility in inward exploration, when they defeat old demons they've long carried with them, when they live more fully, and when they find they can go it alone and no longer need me, but feel caring for me as I have for them. But I do not need them to do any of these things in order for me to feel good about myself or my work or my life.

Another way in which this attitude and relationship are expressed is through what I think of as containment. Here's an example:

CL–23: Jim, I'm going to have to stop coming here! I mean, therapy is just making me worse. I have to either quit therapy or I'll just mess my whole life up. I mean Dick (her husband) is furious with me, and the other day the way I acted at the office, well, they aren't going to put up with that sort of thing.

TH–23: You're really creating problems for yourself everywhere these days, huh?

CL–24: You know it! And I can't seem to stop it. I just fly off at the least little thing.

TH–24: Mm-hum.

CL–25: So you see I've just got to stop coming. Don't you agree?

TH–25: Quitting therapy will solve everything; is that what you're telling me?
CL–26: Oh, no, I suppose not. But what am I going to do?

And so we go. Similarly many client threats of drastic action—suicide, attacks on others, leaving a marriage—need to be heard with a discriminating ear. Such outbursts must never be dismissed, no matter how inflated they may seem. At the same time, there is need to give the client room to say whatever needs to be said without leaping to drastic counteractions. This provides a kind of containment that can allow for relief of emotional pressure without the need or likelihood of actions that could be lastingly damaging. Only that caring presence can make possible an estimate in which reasonable confidence may be reposed as to the degree of risk involved in taking no preventive action about such outbursts.

Changing the Relation and Letting Go of It

Although there are wide differences between the relationship I have with one client and that which I have with another, in general I am inclined to keep a low profile as an individual in the earlier stages and move toward more open disclosure of myself in the latter phases. I feel that too early and too pronounced a disclosure of myself as a person tends to increase the client's difficulty in adopting the inward locus of attention, which is so important. Sometimes, just the opposite is the case, and in those instances the client needs to know me and to know about me to some extent before being able to let go of attention to me and to immerse inwardly. These clients are often those who have had a strong and punishing parent who was unpredictable and thus whom they needed to be wary of at all times. Getting to know me as an individual facilitates their discriminating me from that parent sufficiently to relax their customary vigilance a bit.

As time passes, clients are apt to see me respond more directly and emotionally to their work, and I will make explicit at times my valuing of clients' courage or determination, my pleasure in seeing break-throughs of long resistant walls, or my sharing in their delight at finding larger identities. Because it is less useful to keep the focus *solely* on the clients' inner exploration as they progress, because we have become close in the time we've shared, and because they are often dealing with some of the issues I know in my own life, the latter stages of a client's work often include much more implicit and explicit sharing. By this point too I will sometimes tell about events in my own life which parallel or contrast with those in the client's.

Finally there comes the time of relinquishment. We have grown together a good working relationship; now we must let go of it. This is not a light matter, but it is not a tragic one either. We know that we may see much less of each other; yet we retain warm concern for what we have had and where we will go from here as people. Sometimes we will have further contacts, but inevitably they will be less easy and familiar than we have known when in the routine of our work. Sometimes we will find we want to work through new awkwardness and develop a fresh relationship; sometimes the circumstances of our lives or the places and times of our activities mean that we will rarely if ever see each other again.

The ending needs the authenticity we have sought all along. It can be enriching and freeing when we are straight about it and when we grasp hands in recognition of where we have been and what we have accomplished and in salute to the unknown ahead of us.

A Client's Account of the Caring from the Therapist

The following description is unedited. It conveys the importance to a self-despising person of experiencing that the therapist cares about him. It is my opinion that such caring cannot be enacted but must come genuinely; it is too critically important to risk any deception with it.

> He liked me. Ooof!! Why is it hard to say that, or even write it at this moment? It's such an obvious statement. Trite. Unimportant compared to . . . compared to what, Goddamit? See how I try to dispose of that thought. That offers a clue. "Stay with it." So I shall, but it isn't easy. . . He liked me. I knew it then, I know it now. No, that's not quite correct. At the beginning, as I faced Jim for the first time, I did not know that. In fact, I was quite sure that he wouldn't like me at all. That, as I revealed my-

self, he not only wouldn't like me, but indeed would find me quite disgusting. Just as I did myself. A gloomy, cowardly, inhibited, boring, hypocritical, self-deluding freak. Because that's exactly how I regarded myself. I knew it was hopeless. As soon as he got the picture, as soon as I revealed enough, he would agree. It was just a matter of time. I kept waiting. Each time I revealed some particularly unflattering morsel, I felt: Oh boy! —this is it! This time I've gone too far. . . I knew I could tell when it came—I'd been watching for these things from people for years. I waited. Nothing. Some mistake here? Isn't he paying attention? As if responding to a kind of challenge, I told him more—I placed even more psychic refuse at his feet. Still nothing. If anything, he came closer. What, I thought, is going on here? Is this some kind of hoax? Either he's incredibly talented at hiding his true feelings about me, or. . . I'm backpedaling—avoiding the simple words that are harder to say, what was so important to me was: Does he *like* me? Does he value me? Does he. . . (Ooof!) . . . does he want to be my friend? The feeling comes back to me: Goddamit! What's so important about that?! I'm not here to be *liked*! This man is a psychologist, a PhD, who I'm paying to solve my problems, to figure me out, to understand why my life is such a mess, why. . . I don't give a shit what he feels about me! This is crazy! I don't give a damn if he likes me or hates me or whatever! He can take his feelings about me and shove them right up his . . .

Let's face it. Jim's feelings about me were, and still are, the most important part of our work together. Maybe the only part.

He liked me.

8

Though the Travelers Stop, the Journey Stretches Ahead: The Principal Outcomes of Existential-humanistic Therapy

At last there comes a day of arrival. The journey has brought the travelers to a destination, and that destination is but the threshold of a new phase in their lives. Arrival is an ambivalent thing. There is the joy of completion and the sadness of ending; there is the recognition that the destination arrived at does not ensure a new life (as one had secretly hoped), and there is the realization that new possibilities are available if one will but take hold of them. The streets and squares of the new city are not those of the land left behind, but they are similar, and that is at once reassuring and disappointing. Back of it all is the awareness that the journey still calls; the road is always waiting.

It is familiar to the point of triteness to say that the work of intensive therapy is never completed. Human growth is a dimension without limit. Endings of therapy are always arbitrary. Objective attainments do not dictate when client and therapist will end their partnership. It is a subjective algebra of likely gains against probable costs which each calculates. In the following pages, I describe some typical gains from existential-humanistic psychotherapy which has done its work well and which has been carried toward the upper levels of the scale I set out in the first chapter. No one client is likely to attain all of these nor to realize them in just the way I describe. Each journey is unique, and the rewards won are individual.

The Primacy of the Subjective

When client and therapist have made their journey together well—and that means with struggles, disappointments, setbacks, and conflict as well as with determination, deep affection, penetration into new perceptions, and preparation for their separation—then each comes into a new psychological space. To be sure the therapist has visited this continent before, but seldom does she or he return to the same places in that new land. Meanwhile, the client will often recognize that the realm of the subjective is anciently familiar, even though it has not so clearly been attained before. The essence of this archtypical homeland toward which the psychotherapeutic partners have traveled is the realization of the subjective sovereignty of each human being.

Oh, that's a grand phrasing of it, to be sure. And much that we find at the end of therapy is as mundane and ungrand as paying the bills, going to work, visiting with friends, and hoeing one's garden. Yet, if only we are aware enough, courageous enough, and truly willing, there is the possibility—we can sense—of more. The grand possibility does not demean the everyday; nor does the usual negate the potential our intuition knows (Bugental, 1967c).

Discovery of the Power of Presence

Presence, being here, centeredness, and immediacy—all are terms to point to a fundamental reality. Only in this moment am I alive. All else is in some measure speculative. Only now, *now*, can I make my life different. The client who experiences this fact of great power realizes that its importance goes far beyond the therapeutic office. Roger Walsh (1976), himself a scientist and psychotherapist, describes his experience in this therapy in an insightful account on which I will draw frequently in this chapter. He says of the importance of presence:

> Yet another amazing discovery was the incredible importance of the here and now. I began to be aware that my consciousness is usually divided, with one part focusing on the inner and outer stimuli of the moment and another part fantasizing future or past events. This effectively constitutes a diffusion of consciousness. Furthermore, the internal dialogue, the never-ending, repetitive statements, judging and punishing, etc. occur within this fantasy component of consciousness, and the extent to which this is discarded is the extent to which we are one-pointed and here now. I even reached the point of wondering whether in fact there can be psychological pain if we are completely in the here and now, since psychic pain comes out of comparing what is with what was or what might be (p. 107).

Most of us are truly present in the moment but rarely
Those words circle around a fact of unique and powerful significance. Our usual condition has been called *sleepwalking*, while *being truly awake* is that only occasionally achieved state in which we are in a place of power and from which we may have true governance of our lives. To truly and fully experience one's life and one's concerns in a present-tense, here-and-now, active-voice, first-person way is to bring about an evolution in those concerns. Any other posture is impotent. Only those who come to this recognition through working toward full presence fully appreciate what a fundamental truth is here available.

Searching—The Inner Vision

Many people, when they first come to therapy, are not accustomed to giving serious and continued attention to their subjectivity. Only when emotional pain or other distress enforces such awareness do they attend to their inner processes. Even then, many seek chiefly to have this distraction alleviated so they can get back to the *real world* of objective concerns. But the hidden significance of that word *concerns* is that the world of objectivity is only discovered and given meaning through the operation of subjectivity (Bugental, 1976; Gendlin, 1962). Therapy's insistence on paying attention to the subjective life is the beginning of a pervasive change. One of the results of this process is that the client may begin to experience the centering of life as being within rather than external. That is a profound transition.

The inward sense

A significant outcome of the recentering of one's life is the discovery or increased appreciation of the inward sense. This is an organismic awareness of one's own unique perspective, of whether incoming experience is congenial to one's being, and of what it is that one intends, wants, or seeks to realize. This sense is an expression of one's whole being and is the basis of an inner solidity and orientation in living (see Bugental, 1976, Chapter 1).

Many people learned early in life to disregard the inward sense (what Maslow, 1967, called the *impulse voices*). Typically, such people find it hard to make decisions they can live with, to take actions that are truly satisfying, to develop plans on which they can follow through with dedication. The inward sense makes possible discriminations among potential experiences, selectivity of perception, continuity of enterprise, and ongoing guidance of one's own activities. It is not some mystical, extrasensory power; it is the totality of our awareness, functioning out of our being truly present in our own lives.

The searching process which we gave so central a place in our therapeutic conception is a channeled use of the inward sense. When therapy has helped a person come to use that searching skill, there is a lasting access to inner awareness and thus the potential to enrich life long after the therapy is terminated.

A client's description

Walsh (1976) writes,

> One of the most wondrous discoveries of all was the slowly

> dawning awareness of the presence of a formerly subliminal, continuously changing stream of inner experience. The range, richness, Heraclitean, and awesome nature of this internal universe amazed and continues to amaze me. Here was an ever-present, but formerly unsuspected veritable internal universe. After a couple of months, I began to perceive more clearly a constant flux of visual images. One of the most exciting of many exciting memories is that of the sudden recognition that these images exquisitely symbolized what I was feeling and experiencing in each moment. Here was a previously unsuspected gold mine of information about myself and the meaning of my experiences (pp. 100–101).

Releasing Latent Potential

To be really centered in one's subjectivity with full presence is to discover conveniently at hand much that is ordinarily unavailable. Mental contents of a kind often regarded as unconscious—memories, impulses, and fantasies usually denied or represented only symbolically—are accessible. The search process has demonstrated that control and choice are greater when consciousness is open, and one now knows that undesired acts need not automatically issue from acceptance of their impulses into awareness. Obviously a person who has this sort of internal climate has a broader base for choice making, for mobilizing energy, and for putting decisions into effective action. Walsh speaks of the "incessant reality distorting nature of the 'internal dialogue' and the trap of believing that this dialogue . . . represent(s) reality."

Most of us spend so much of our powers wrestling with a phantom existence, made up of self-criticism, comparisons with others, apprehensions and expectations for the future, relentless and unrealistic demands for improvement, excuses for failures, and similar life-sapping thoughts and feelings. As this destructive and self-betraying inner harangue lessens, energy and vitality become available. Walsh reports "one unexpected but greatly appreciated change was an increase in energy (and) I began reducing my sleep needs." Effectively, this is equivalent to lengthening life. A similar result comes as we experience time freshly.

Changed Time Sense

Customary ways of seeing time accord the clock the keeping of "real" time while suspecting subjective time of distortion. In the same way, conventional experience sees time as flying when one is enjoying life but as dragging during boredom or pain. But those who work their ways to greater centeredness of life give quite different reports, as does Walsh:

> One of the first effects was time dilation. Formerly I had gone through life attempting to withdraw attention immediately after any completed act. However, the therapy experience of reflection produced a similar change in awareness outside the therapy situation, and I soon found myself examining my experience more closely. The subjective effect of this was to dramatically increase the amount of subjective experience, such that I felt my life had expanded by a factor of two or three times and I now felt as though twice as much was happening in each day, a very pleasant experience (p. 100).

Time is not fixed, constant, or independent of the human (as the physicists are also recognizing). Clients accomplish amounts in clock time that is far too brief. They can telescope experience that usually requires hours into minutes. Similarly, an occasion of great pleasure or satisfaction may be experienced as stretching over many hours while the clock shows but little elapsed, objective time. Conversely, faced with a necessary but unpleasant situation—e.g., oral surgery—the client reports that it seemed to take but a few minutes while the clock registered well over an hour.

Summary: Subjective Sovereignty

My own experience and that of those whom I accompany convince me that a great deal of the distress which so many people experience may be traced in no small part to our living as exiles from our own homeland, the inner world of subjective experience. Through psychotherapy, we can overcome the social conditioning which has taught us to be suspicious and guilty about living from the center out, about truly putting internal wholeness at the highest priority, and about making choices in terms of inner sensing of our own unique needs and wants. When we have gained that liberation, the whole experience of being alive can be subtly different. We know our own individuality; we find richness within our own flow of awareness; we deal with issues and concerns with greater integrity, and we find the possibility of creative and aesthetic participation of life

The heart of the matter is simple, fundamental, and often totally overlooked—*the true home of each of us is in inner experiencing.* Thus the true mission of psychotherapy is to affect that experiencing in ways which improve the quality of life for the person. Symptoms are superficial. Whether a particular symptom is eliminated, changed, or unaffected is secondary to whether the person having that symptom experiences more vitality, potency, and opportunity in life. Behavior changes are by-products. Whether a specific behavior pattern continues unaffected, is replaced, or is modified is trivial in contrast to whether the person having that pattern discovers more dignity, choice, and personal meaningfulness in life.

Our homeland is within, and there we are sovereign. Until we discover that ancient fact anew and uniquely for each of us as an individual, we are condemned to wander seeking solace where it cannot be found, in the outer world.

Changes in Life Experience

Changed Expectancy of Life

Most us carry around a model of life which we've put together without much thought and which may look something like this: When we are children our main task is to learn enough to be adults. By our early 20s we should be ready to meet most life situations; although we may need to pick up a few additional learnings—e.g., in relation to jobs or children. Adult life is a matter of living out a reasonable program for life which mature and mentally O.K. people have worked out. If unusual stresses hit, then special help such as psychotherapy may be needed. Of course, bad feelings, such as fear, anxiety, pain, anger, etc., are signals that something is wrong, since normal people don't have such feelings, or at least only very occasionally or mildly.

That model is almost totally wrong, and it is damnably destructive. Most of us know that, but an awful lot of us still let it operate in the dark of our unexamined assumptions and intentions for our lives. Effective psychotherapy brings light into those recesses and thus frees life to be vital and authentic.

Reclaiming Our Emotional Inheritance

Emotions are regarded ambivalently in that distorted model. To be sure, the happier feelings are generally welcomed, although even then with suspicion by more than a few people. More than one supposedly wise person has lamented the influence of the emotions on human affairs. Yet emotions are the essential cement of a full and meaningful life.

It is easy to recognize the importance of the emotions as signals to call our attention to things going wrong or to assure us that all is well. It is familiar to recognize that emotions give color and texture to life, and analogies to sunshine and shadow are trite. Psychotherapy reinforces such common wisdom, but psychotherapy points farther.

Emotions are part of the fabric of human relationships. What we do and what we experience matter to ourselves and to those with whom we relate. That fabric of human connectedness means that our identities don't stop with our separate envelopes of skin, but extend to the perimeters of our caring. Caring is the general form of the particular experiences which are our feelings. The emotionless person is isolated by the very choice that denied the affective dimension of being.

Seeking to avoid unwanted emotions, we suffer the fading of the wanted feelings as well. Emotions are not so many packages of breakfast food lined up on the shelf, separate and unitary. *Emotionality is a unitary dimension of being;* one suppresses one aspect at the cost of crippling all. Suppressed emotionality is suppressed, shrunken living. To be alive is to know joy and sorrow, pride and guilt, hope and fear. Too often we feel shame or dismay when we have such feelings, letting that false model persuade us that they signal something wrong in our nature. Psychotherapy discloses the illusion and relieves the secondary distress. Therapy aids us in finding a larger capacity for caring, for depth, for emotionality.

Psychotherapy teaches also that *an emotional episode is an incident not a lasting condition,* and this relieves unnecessary distress for many. Clients often feel that if they were to let go to their anger or their grief, for example, they would never recover perspective. Quite the contrary is the case. Once there is an adequate release of pent-up feeling, then a natural evolution of the emotion takes place. The person who fears emotion will take over blocks this evolution and thus is already taken over by the emotion of fear.

Changed Life Intentions

As the pain of one's distress is lessened and some sense of gaining a foothold on a different way of life emerges, the client begins questioning goals and plans that have been previously unexamined. For a great many people, therapy is the first genuine and prolonged opportunity to ask the question, "What do I really want to do with the fact of being alive?" Asking that question can be explosive. One may find life is blindly following what is expected rather than what is chosen. One may discover with shock that parental patterns—often even those consciously rejected—are determining how one uses time, money, relationships, emotions, and life itself.

Outdated life intentions exposed to the light of current presence wither rapidly and their places may be taken by current goals for life, goals which express who one more truly is. Instead of unwittingly living out a childhood script derived from parents and others, one may take charge of being and find the possibility of actualizing one's own potential is at last at hand.

Changed Life Pace

A frequent outcome of therapy is the client's discovering that self-alienation has led to a life similar to that of a prisoner who is driven by a suspicious and relentless keeper. The person, split into a tyrant boss and an untrustworthy worker, continually strives to do more, to do it better, and to prove self against an impossible standard. Walsh (1976) describes this pattern.

> Formerly my belief had been the constant self-monitoring, judging, and harsh goading were essential if I was to motivate myself toward desired goals. The internal state was, as my therapist put it so often and so nicely, "a master-slave relationship in which you have to be constantly watching and on guard against yourself." The counterproductive nature of this state of

> affairs eventually became apparent, and I began to realize that harsh judgments, anger, and disappointment in myself only fueled the negativity that I regretted (p. 102).

Many creative professional and artistic people share the apprehension that they will become indolent and unproductive if they do not drive themselves. Once they recognize the self-contradiction of having to make sure they do what they want to do, there is a marked reduction in tension and often an increase in productivity which is personally meaningful.

Reduced striving

Eastern disciplines have taught many of us in the west to look askance at our culture's great emphasis on striving, competing, achieving, and producing. We recognize increasingly that this mood destroys much that is rich and meaningful in life. Nevertheless we find it hard to free ourselves, and more than one person has fallen into the paradox of trying hard not to try hard. Walsh describes the way in which this paradox may be resolved when one stays centered and aware.

> Gradually it began to dawn that perhaps I didn't have to feel so "active" and "doing" in getting things done. There was also the discovery that inner emotional problems didn't necessarily have to be "worked on or worked out," but that I could at least sometimes simply witness them and watch their evolution and resolution. This sense has increased to a point where I now wonder whether the sense of "doing" may not actually be an illusion (p. 106).

Striving, doing, trying, and such urgencies tend, for the most part, to be products of the master and slave split. Wholeness of being has no place in its truly subjective perspective for such self-manipulation. This is the truth behind the frequent injunction in meditative disciplines to "let go." It is the self which must be relinquished; then one's fundamental unity may be realized.

Lessened narcotized living

Immediately related to the reduction in striving which comes with greater subjective centering is a reduction in need for psychological anesthetics. Much, but by no means all, of TV, radio, motion pictures, commercial spectator sports, gambling, and many other "entertainment" offerings in our culture may be seen as ways of affording the essentially passive viewer a narcotic to suppress the anxiety of living or to mask the emptiness of being an object. Walsh speaks of finding himself "escaping into mindless activities less often (e.g., listening to the radio) and being more willing to 'hang out' with my experience and my mind."

Increased appreciation of experience

As Walsh suggests, becoming more centered leads to valuing subjectivity much more and this accompanies and stimulates discovery of the unlimited richness latent within each person.

> As I spent more time tuning into my experience, my perceptual sensitivity increased. The absolute threshold seemed to decrease and discriminative abilities to increase. Initially this change seemed particularly localized to internal percepts, but it gradually became apparent that it also included heightened sensitivity to external stimuli . . . as the sensitivity to the inner experiential stream increased, so did its recognized richness until it soon assumed a psychedelic quality which I had previously thought to be only attainable with drugs (pp. 101–2).

Changed Perspective on Human Relationships

As may be anticipated, the person who comes into greater subjective centering in life relates more meaningfully and selectively with others. Much of our ordinary socializing has the same narcotizing quality which we noted in talking about entertainment forms. Small talk is familiarly damned; yet it may be recognized as more authentic in some ways than apparently more serious or profound talk. Social chit-chat seldom pretends to be other than a space filler; while much talk in academic, business, and other more sober settings is destructive in its unthinking objectification of human experience and its bland assumption that the objective world is the only truly important arena of life. An atmosphere filled with disguised competition for power over others' lives, with grasping for money and possessions, with heedless mutilations and assassinations of hopes and dreams—whether in a board room, a faculty club, a church council, or a social agency staff meeting—is more polluted and more poisonous for human life than a smog-filled city.

Coming home to one's native land of subjective centeredness nearly always means some reduction in attachment to familiar goals such as wealth, possessions, prestige, offices, and notoriety. Some people simply drop out at this point, relinquishing the world and devoting themselves to inward explorations. If they are criticized for not contributing directly to the social weal, they may also be defended as doing less harm than many who are in the midst of things. Ultimately such dropouts, perhaps, contribute to greater sanity of human experience. But there are not a few others who go on to express their underlying allegiance to humankind through becoming in subtle or obvious ways change agents, seeking with individuals or groups to bring about that change of consciousness which it is increasingly agreed must occur if our species is to survive and have any possibility of achieving its destiny (Bugental, 1967a, 1970, 1971a and b).

Once the subjective perspective is realized, it becomes manifest that so much of our lives is tragically wasted in fighting demons, which are of our own creation, which are the products of our alienation from our own being, and which are fully overcome only when denied the sustenance of our fear and antagonism. That triumph comes not from combat, but from opening our awareness to our true natures and dispelling the enemy with the light of authentic being. The ominous and inescapable truth is that our cultural institutions are failing seriously—church, courts, government, schools, and social agencies, all are proving inadequate to the demands of our time. Each of those agencies is founded in important degree on our fear and mistrust of our own natures. Alienated from our selves, we erect defenses which further estrange us and then inevitably set about circumventing those very agencies to assert our rebellious, sovereign identity. Just so does the client throw up barriers against the conditions of being human and then need to layer additional defenses, while questing again and again to find freedom.

A tragic sense of life

One looks from the perspective of subjective centeredness upon human life with a sense of tragedy. Walsh says, "I was able to look back at my own life, at the lives of others, and at some of society's and psychiatry's norms as narrowly and tragically founded in ignorance and fear." This need not be a perspective of futility and uninvolvement, but it is very likely a posture of nonattachment, in the sense of not buying into the distortions revealed by this view. One cannot see the human experience in this way without feeling sadness at the great effort of so many to be as they think they should be, at the tremendous caring which somehow is manifested on every side in the midst of so much that is despairing, at the immense outpouring of hope and dedication of which so much is foredoomed because it is so unaware.

It is not that the person who has achieved a measure of subjective sovereignty feels ready to be a new Messiah; usually, quite to the contrary, there is a general feeling of humility before the enormous issues confronting human beings and the astonishing achievements that have been made. The only special perspective is the recognition that there is an absolutely essential first step which is being almost totally overlooked. Until men and women accept their own natures and fully realize that they are the authors, not the victims, of their destinies, all their efforts are foredoomed. So long as human beings mistrust themselves and found their attempts to improve their lot upon antagonism to their own natures, those attempts can be nothing but antagonistic to their creators. This is the tragedy of the human situation.

Enlarged Sense of Identity

Repeatedly in preceding pages I've talked about helping my client attain a larger sense of identity. Just what does that mean? Every person lives implicitly in terms of a largely implicit and unexamined image of her or his own nature. This image says what is possible and what is impossible for the person to do; it describes what the world around offers that can help and what threats it contains, and it sets forth what is desirable and what is to be avoided. It is my belief that most of us carry images of a creature with limited capacities, with only moderate endurance and potential, and with a destiny to be more done to than to be a doer. The enlarged sense of identity potential to human beings is that of being a great deal more able to bring about the experiences they truly want to have, of living in the midst of a treasure house of vitality within their own consciousnesses, and of continually shaping the world and their own natures. Walsh describes discovering "a sense of power which I really revelled in after a lifetime of feeling inferior."

Me, Myself, and I

It will help to convey what is possible in enlarging one's sense of identity if we consider ways of distinguishing between a person's identity and the person's "self." That distinction is confusing when one has not previously considered the matter. The children's chant, "Me, myself, and I" reveals the common assumption that these three words are synonyms. I believe this is not so. I think they point to quite importantly different aspects of being.

> *Me* is a word used to designate an object of perception, something which we can experience (as contrasted with the experiencing of that object). Thus *me* includes my physical body, my customary patterns of behavior (as an observer might see them), and my memories of past actions, feelings, and events in my life. The *me* of itself is inert, is unaware, has no power. The *me* is a construction of the *I* and has no life of its own.

In all, the me is quite a different thing than a synonym for who *I* am. The me is the automobile; it is not the principle of internal combustion, nor is it the process of moving through space, and certainly it is not the driver. The me is the moving trees and grasses; it is not the wind which moves them. The me is an object; it is not the subject.

Similarly, the *self* is an object.

> *Self* is a word used with some overlapping of meaning with the word *me*. The common element abstracted out of many and varied perceptions of one's *me* may be named the *self*. This makes its significance synonymous with the *self-concept* (Raimy, 1948; Bugental, 1952), and this will be my usage. The *self* is the distillation of one's past experiences of one's own being and of conscious and unconscious hopes and fears for one's being now and in the future.

We construct, each of us, a *self* as a record of who we have been, and we mistakenly confuse that record for a prescription for who we can be. Without attention to our inward sensing, we make choices and undertake courses of action in terms of what we have done in the past, and then we often find that our choices are unsatisfying and our actions are not invested with full commitment. Because I have long enjoyed reading science-fiction does not mean that I will most enjoy this new space opera on the television tonight. I need to attend inwardly to find what my genuine wanting is now. But who is this *I* who needs so to attend?

> *I-process* is a term to designate the subject of one's being, the be-ing-ness of a human life. *I-process* is a communication device to refer to that which is purely subject as though it were object so that we can talk about it. (This is ultimately a contradiction, for when we talk about something we make it the object of discussion, and being an object is the one thing a subject cannot be.) The *I-process* is the person be-*ing*, which is expressed through the person's act-ing, speak-ing, and so on.

This is a confusing but very important point. We are so accustomed to dealing with objects that the very idea of something purely subjective is hard to grasp, and as already indicated it is beyond the possibility of verbal grasp. (The word "grasp" again points to our language's limitation to the world of objects in which we are accustomed to laying hands on—grasping—ideas as well as things.) We cannot see our I-processes anymore than our eyes can see themselves, for those I-processes are the very process of the seeing. To look into a mirror is to see the reflection of our eyes as they were a microsecond ago; to seek awareness of our subjectivity in watching our thoughts or actions is to see what we left behind just a moment ago (Bugental, 1975–76).

Nothingness

When I begin to realize that my truest identity is as process and not as fixed substance, I am on the verge of a terrible emptiness and a miraculous freedom. The nothingness of being, the transitoriness of substance, the endless possibilities of awareness are so shocking to recognize that often the sensations are those of vertigo, anxiety, and denial. The familiar fear of death and oblivion is but one form of this most existential of confrontations. We feel lost in space without any sense of direction and bereft of all comfort so long as we persist in seeking a given identity or a preexisting form for our existence. Yet, that is exactly what we feel compelled to do over and over again.

> Very well, I can see that I am not this body, these habits I've built up, or even my profession or my family relationships. I can see that each of those parts of what I've always thought of as my identity could be replaced by quite other parts. I could have a female body instead of my man's shape; could have developed quite other ways of talking and even thinking; could have gone into another field of work or married differently, of course. But if I think, not of replacing each of these with something else, but of relinquishing all such parts of who I am without any substitutions, then . . . Then . . . Then I am frightened and clawing at the walls of my nothingness, whimpering before the impassivity of silence.

As frightening as this recognition of our nothingness (see Friedman, 1967; Hammer, 1971; Novak, 1970 for further studies of this experience and its meanings), still another comes soon after. We begin to realize that the world which has been the solid foundation of our being is equally a construction of our awareness. We have learned from infancy to see it a certain way, and although we alter that some over the years, essentially we accept what we have been taught and believe that to be the intrinsic nature of being. It is not; it is our construction. Other peoples experience the world differently. No longer can we in the west so blithely and blindly assume that these people are just less intelligent, less scientific, or less developed than we. They have built their worlds in quite other but equally valid ways. Today we are at last casting off our provincialism and coming to respect those other visions of being. Others (Castaneda, 1968, 1971, 1972, 1974; Deikman, 1976; Lilly, 1972; McGlashan, 1967, Ram Dass, 1974; Van Dusen, 1972) tell of other visions and of our own growing recognition of the possibilities for seeing ourselves and our worlds differently.

Freedom

It is only after we begin genuinely confronting and incorporating the recognitions that our own identities are solely as processes and that world is the quite arbitrary construction of our awarenesses that we can move toward discovering and appreciating the freedom thus opened to us. If I am but the process of my being, then I can, and indeed must, remake my life each moment, and I can choose to make it quite different than it has been in the past, for the past is no longer the master of this present moment.

> As I write these words, I can pause to have a cup of tea and to listen to some music on the record player, or I can keep on writing.
>
> As I write these words, I can suddenly begin writing gibberish—canteloupe is aired by blue graphite when glacking dorts press on the geefers—or I can keep on with my usual writing.
>
> As I write these words, I can suddenly throw over the typewriter and table, stand up and announce that it's just too damn much work trying to write all this, and I'm going to go to a movie instead; or I can keep on writing.
>
> As I write these words, I can decide that all I've written is shallow and insufficient, that I must simply stop all other activity and devote myself to a great deal more study of the great thinkers before presuming to write another line, or I can keep on writing.
>
> As I write these words, I can push aside the typewriter and go get my wife and my daughter and announce that we're going to get out of this way of living, that we'll put the house on the market, close out our practice, muster what resources we can, and go live in an isolated mountain community where we'll try to get back to the most basic levels of being; or I can keep on writing.
>
> As I write these words, I can get up from the typewriter, put a few things in a knapsack, say nothing to anyone, go out the door, take the older car, and head out in just any direction, live by my wits, make no relationships, indulge every impulse, and when life gets too anguish-filled, kill myself; or I can keep on writing.

Each minute the choice. Freedom and trade-offs. Each possibility has something to make it inviting, but each has some costs. I weigh one against the other, and I choose. And I choose. And I choose . . .

Feeling Greater Power in Life

As my examples have just demonstrated, one has at every moment an immense range of potential selves from which to choose. The power to make this choice is intrinsic in our being. We so often deny it, but when we open ourselves to the awareness, we feel a sense of greater potency and commitment even when we continue to do what we were going to do before. And often we choose a fresh course, for we see that the trade-offs are not so formidable when really weighed, and we realize that we are not so fragile either. Awaking to current reality, to our matured being, we often see that we've unthinkingly been acting as though the limits of childhood and dependency still contained us. Or we may discover that we have blindly repeated old ways of doing even though they are manifestly unsuccessful. In so many ways, discovering our freedom means the possibility of letting go of self-defeating patterns long maintained.

But this greater feeling of power in one's own life can yield other gains than those associated with overcoming past distresses. As the quotation from Walsh (pp. 122–123) described, there is the discovery of the richness of the inner world, the endless possibilities it brings forth, and even the kinds of experiences which we've long thought depended on artificial stimulants—e.g., synesthesia and psychedelic-like imagery and feelings. Additional kinds of potency in one's own being are described by Walsh:

> About this time I also began to find that it was possible to transmute emotions, and that something like fear could be changed to excitement. . . Not surprisingly, as these preceding discoveries and processes began "to take," I found myself experiencing more joy than I'd ever believed possible. . . Towards the end of therapy, the incredible power of beliefs and models to function as self-fulfilling prophecies began to become apparent. . . The extent to which I, and I suspect all of us, underestimate the power of our beliefs staggered me (p. 107).

Lessened vulnerability

I've already referred to the discovery that many of us make that we have expended great effort or given up desired experiences to ward off distresses which upon examination in the light of current life would not be so great as to warrant such sacrifices. In the same way we come to realize that some pain surely comes to each of us from time to time and that choosing a course of action which will give us some much wanted result is well worth some discomfort accompanying it. Helen hesitated to ask for a raise at work because her superior might think her too concerned with money, but when she brought out her feelings fully she realized that this would be at most a trifling embarrassment compared to the increased enjoyment a long overdue pay raise would provide. Pete avoided taking a professional examination he was sure that he could pass because he couldn't be certain to do it perfectly, a standard for his own performance which could be set aside when he weighed the negligible pain of just doing "well enough" against the delay in getting on with his career. Toby continually dodged arguments with his wife, fearing the pain of conflict with her, until he recognized how the inauthenticity of their relationship was actually more hurtful to both of them.

Drawing on Inner Wisdom

Our identities are as subjects, and thus they are invisible. We are most truly the seeing, not that which is seen. We are the knowing, not what is known. We are the process of being aware, not the content of the awar-ing. Awareness is not measurable in objective terms. We cannot say how much is in awareness or what its shape or dimensions. All such descriptions would make awareness into an object, which it is not. We can talk about memory and its contents, for memory is really only evidenced by its contents. So it is too with consciousness; it is evidenced by what it is we are conscious of, and thus we can talk about how much we are conscious of.

The searching process, which has been so central to what I described in earlier chapters, is a means for bringing materials into consciousness. It is a way of exploring awareness, like a flashlight probing a dark attic and picking out first one item and then another. Clearly there is much more potential in awareness than we are conscious of at any time. Whether there is, in the ideal state, any limit to awareness is an unanswerable question. Indeed, it may not even be a sensible question, since awareness is not in the same dimension of being as are limits and contents.

The searching process, as we saw, works best when it is motivated solely by a sense of concern and an expectancy of discovery. It is interfered with when one engages in problem-solving and conscious guidance. The searching process is best the more subjectively it is used. The things that interfere with it do so by making it the object of manipulation. Thus it is no longer truly subjective, and it becomes limited to the objective consciousness.

When the searching process is freed of this constraint, it seems to be expressing a deeper and unconscious wisdom at work. This way of describing it is, almost certainly, distortive, for once again it is making a subjective process into an objective entity, a fund of wisdom. But the point is that again and again clients who learn to use the searching process will find themselves thinking of things, experiencing feelings, and coming to recognitions which were quite unpredictable in any conscious way before they began searching.

> Brad started the hour talking about his struggle with himself while driving to the office. On the one hand he wanted to develop an "agenda" for us to deal with; on the other he knew he would use the time better to discover in the moment his genuine concerns. As he talked, he found himself thinking of his father's continual admonishing and chidings whenever Brad, as a child, tried to do anything. With many protestations of love and wanting to help, the father had implicitly conveyed the idea that Brad just couldn't be counted on to do on his own what he should do. Brad realized that he was repeating the same pattern within himself, and then abruptly—in a gush of tears and pain—he recognized that he was now repeating it still with his own son. This is the skeleton of the hour's work. It took many turnings which importantly rounded out the exploration and gave promise that Brad's inner vision would permeate many parts of his life, such as his relations with subordinates at work, with his wife, and with friends.

Thus Walsh speaks of "an increasing faith in our inner wisdom and guidance" and again later on says, "As my faith in this [inner] source of knowledge increased, I began to gain an appreciation of the saying that 'the answers are available inside', and also that the growth experience is one of recognizing what we already know. This sense of the presence of inner wisdom was a very beautiful one."

Accepting Our God-nature

> As these feelings and awareness deepened, there came a dawning recognition of what I can only call our God-like nature. Feelings and experiences don't just happen, but are actively created by us; then we live in them and almost always we lose ourselves in them, forgetting who is their creator. This awesome recognition frightened me in therapy, and I think that I suppressed most of my awareness of it and still do to a large extent since its implications are literally mind-boggling. On those rare occasions when I do confront them, I experience fear in the recognition of our incredible power and our aloneness in it (Walsh, p. 108).

To me, God is a word used to point to our ineffable subjectivity, to the unimaginable potential which lies within each of us, to the aspirations which well up within us for greater truth and vividness of living, to our compassion for the tragedy of the human condition, to our pride in the undestroyed but endlessly assaulted dignity of our being, and to something more. To the sense of mystery within which we always live if we are truly aware and to the dedication to explore that mystery which is the very essence of being human.

In another setting (Bugental, 1976, Chapter 8), I said that we human beings take our sense of God from our deepest intuitions as to what is ultimate in our own depths. This is a view born of my own inner searching, of course, and it has been supported by the discoveries of people with whom I've traveled toward the transcendent levels of therapeutic/growth outcomes.

The idealized image and our God-nature

This observation of the deep convergence of what is human and what is divine needs to be distinguished from the idealized (but alienated) self image, which I several times referred to in earlier pages. Both of these conceptions have to do with the positive potentials of human beings, but one enlightens living and one burdens it. The idealized image blights life and destroys fulfillment, for it contrasts all that is actual with an impossible standard. Realization of our God-potential, on the other hand, illuminates our daily living by putting it under the aspect of eternity, as Maslow (1971) loved to say.

The person who learns to live from the center, who is open to the searching of awareness, who accepts into full consciousness what is disclosed in that process, and who keeps faith with all being is in touch with potentials far beyond those we ordinarily experience. Some accounts of apparently miraculous events (e.g. Castaneda, 1974; Ram Dass, 1974) are very likely based on the actualization of such possibilities.

A client's own account

Chapter 6 ended with an excerpt from a client's account of the experience of being in therapy. In that portion quoted, the client was describing his inward searching and the panic to which it led. I will again quote the last few sentences of the earlier excerpt and then add a further portion of the client's account:

> As I tuned into the uneasiness, it built and built until it was almost a panic. As I struggled to stay with it and not run away, its essence began to become clear to my consciousness. It became apparent to me that I was afraid of not existing. The question that I was confronted with directly was, "If I let go of my sense of I—John Cogswell, my belief that there is a me that I call I, what will there be?" At the moment that this question became clear, it was also crystally clear to me that "John Cogswell" and "I" were just mental concepts. I also knew from my experience of letting go in the past that if I stayed with it and went through the center of the storm—went into and faced the very worst of it—that I would emerge in a new place with an increased sense of aliveness. I had been through many of these death and rebirth cycles. So, based upon the faith that I would emerge again, I let go of the concept of "I" and faced the possibility of total death, total nothingness. What happened was the most profound experience of my whole life to that point. I became aware of everything being pure light, everything—just plain everything was a pure radiant loving light—a living life of pure love. It was immediately clear that this omnipresence of living Love was God and that everything, including me was part of it. There was a me that existed beyond the personal life of concepts called "John Cogswell." And that me was a living Love that is part of God. Futhermore, there was an immediate awareness of life existing at various levels of vibration. At the level of my personal life, there

> was a slower vibration and from that level there were higher and higher levels of vibration being. And, in some sense I didn't understand, there seemed to be crystallization into some kind of form or entity at each of these levels. There was, with all of this experiencing, a deep sense of peace and tranquillity. When I finally opened my eyes I had a totally different relationship to life. All sense of self-consciousness and separateness was gone. I was not only me, I was Jim, I was everyone. The words "I" and "you" no longer made sense. There was no separation. No duality—only oneness. I also became aware that living this greater life I had a sense of knowing the life of the people with me who were really me also. I could live them directly.

This is one eminently sane, scientifically trained, and completely responsible person's vision of the further potential of human life (Cogswell, 1977). The quotation from Walsh given earlier is from a man who is a recognized scientist. Each of them, and I and others, have caught glimpses of the farther potential of being. It is not to be expected that all glimpses will be the same. It is important that this vision, this dream, be respected and allowed to put our lives into a greater perspective.

The Impossible Dream

What is easily overlooked is that there is a constructive aspect to dreaming the impossible dream as well as a destructive possibility. If one turns on oneself with hatred and punishing abuse for not achieving the impossible then the destructive potential is being realized. But if one uses the sense of ultimate possibility to give one touch with what is most profound in life and to orient one's journey toward what is valued, then the dream enriches, brings comfort, and inspires.

Happiness, that most elusive, of temptresses, is not to be won by direct pursuit. Happiness arises when one experiences that the actuality of life is not gravely less than one had expected. The impossible dream, when it is constructively held, is not an expectancy but a guiding vision. Thus one's happiness does not depend on achieving that dream.

Satisfaction, happiness's sister, is sought in vain through accumulating possessions or recognitions. Satisfaction is gained when one has the feeling that one's own efforts are making a difference in one's life in relation to that dream. Satisfaction does not require that we achieve the dream either; it only calls for us to be experiencing our own powers in moving toward that vision. This is no call for striving, let it be understood. The vision may be that of Nirvana or Satori; the dream may be that of nonattachment.

The dream of being God is the dream of being most truly what we are. Debunking (Maslow's "desacrilizing", 1967) has over-carried. Human beings may not be the center of the objective universe—whatever such a concept may mean. Human beings must certainly recognize at last that each is the center of a subjective universe. We are God. By despising, mistrusting, and trying to harness ourselves, we are bringing our race to the brink of destruction. We are God; valuing, trusting, and realizing ourselves; we may yet preserve the possibilities which are latent in our very being.

The word "God" is not a familiar one in texts on psychotherapy. Perhaps it is time for it to become so. It's a different word than we had thought in our childhoods, and it's a different world in which we use that word. We are not the creatures we imagined. We can become the creators of what will be. Possibility is open in all directions.

Some Frontier Speculations

The practice of existential-humanistic psychotherapy provides one with a continually intriguing vista on human experience. For me, one of the most consistent recognitions has been how far that experience outruns the theories and descriptions we propound for it and how incredibly more vast it is than the prevailing image of humankind, which is implicit in most of our social forms such as government, education, and religion. We cast our institutions for Lilliputians and try to contort ourselves to fit those shrunken dimensions. I will try to illustrate my meaning by a few quick sketches of areas in which I believe further human potential resides, areas which are by and large not accepted by our prevailing view of our own natures.

Intersubjective communication

I believe that we all use what is called *telepathy* continually without recognizing it. Certainly two people who are intimately involved with each other—lovers, parent and child, therapist and client—often come to take for granted that the words they exchange are but a portion of their communication. Even strangers, if *en rapport*, often communicate a great deal beyond the explicit meaning of their words. We have tended to explain these communications with words such as empathy, minimal cues, common associations, and so on, and surely all of these function to aid the exchange of meanings and feelings. But beyond these, we need to recognize how much ideas, images, and even specific words may be transmitted between people without dependence solely on objective media.

As clients arrive at more open awareness of being, they often report heightened ability to sense where their companions are at, to exchange thoughts, to anticipate what will be said, and so on. It is increasingly evident that the envelope of the skin does not contain all that is the being, and that our beingness is a shared matter when we are free to let it flow out with others.

The possibility of awareness beyond physical death

This is a touchy subject, heavily laden with emotional prejudices on all sides. Only a few years ago it was considered the mark of naiveté or of neurosis even to speculate about the possibility that consciousness might continue after bodily death. The fashion—and it was that—was to insist on oblivion as the only outcome. Today we are less dogmatic, less certain here as in so many areas. Increasingly there are suggestions (Kübler-Ross, 1969, Moody, 1975) that we have closed the books prematurely. More than one of my clients, as they have moved toward the transpersonal—and quite without our ever discussing the matter—have come to a conviction of the continuation of awareness in some form. This is a matter, of course, on which I cannot make any definitive statement, but I am struck with how the recognition of the constructional nature of self and world naturally leads us toward a sense of being that goes beyond the body as the sole repository of awareness.

Healing and health

It has been familiar for a third of a century that mental and emotional processes could cause *psychosomatic ailments*. The body was vulnerable to our psyches, we were told repeatedly. But only in the last five to ten years has the benign influence of the psychological upon the physical become respectable in other than certain religious sects. Now the healing potential of our intentionality is modishly in the focus of popular attention.

Watching clients free themselves from neurotic encumbrances and shrunken identities, I have noted again and again how the body becomes an instrument on which the person plays the music of life. At times this is the sad, discordant sound of inner conflict and anxiety, and the body is stiff and breathing is shallow. At these points colds are frequent, muscles respond erratically, and digestion and elimination are undependable. Emotional pain is often echoed in physical distress; psychic cramping is mirrored in clutched up posture and vital processes.

As the person begins to free life of these distortions, the body again expresses what is happening. Breathing becomes deeper, movement is more fluid and graceful, and the vital systems function more peacefully.

There is a further process on which I have less observational evidence but about which I am coming to some degree of conviction nevertheless. I believe it is possible for the intentionality of a person to be mobilized to arrest, or even in some instances to reverse, pathological processes. I think that the person who has learned to get truly centered, to call upon the deeper wisdom I've described, and to focus concern with an open expectancy has a powerful means for combating organic illness. I anticipate that in time we will learn to facilitate that process even further, and I salute those pioneers now doing the difficult task of exploring this ground (see, for example, Mischlov, 1975; Samuels and Samuels, 1975).

9

The Journey Over, the Guide Reflects: What Being a Therapist Means in My Own Life

Traveler and guide separate, go their separate ways, tell their individual stories to their friends. Each has been and always will remain a special person to the other, but time and distance take their levies. Gradually the memories grow less vivid, and new activities and relationships become central. But there are the times of recollection and reflection still.

In this final chapter, I will say something of what this profession has meant to me. It is not possible to describe that experience fully in words, but I'll try to convey some of the flavor of the therapist's life as I know it.

Psychotherapy in the forms most familiar today is largely a

very recent phenomenon. In my own lifetime—and I by no means feel ancient yet—it has emerged from a little known practice chiefly concerned with the severely disturbed to a mainstream part of the culture. The literature of the discipline has proliferated unbelievably. In the 1940s and early 1950s, one could own most of the books on the subject and not have them take up much shelf-space. Today there is no likelihood of a person keeping pace with the flood of books, journals, audio and video tapes, announcements of workshops and lectures, and much more that sweeps over our desks.

Once the realm of *mental therapy* was chiefly occupied by psychoanalysis on the one hand or a kind of rational advising on the other. We have already recognized the great array of therapies now available. In my earlier days in the field, psychiatrists were the only ones who were supposed to engage in this kind of treatment. Today psychologists, social workers, counselors of all backgrounds, ministers, educational professionals, paraprofessionals with extensive or little preparation, and nearly everyone else does a bit of therapy.

I need to express my concern about this last matter: I think working with people in need of help in their lives is a very serious trust. I know that many kinds of experiences can be *therapeutic*, but I feel that a distinction needs to be made as to what is truly *therapy*. To be sure, there are many legitimately trained, fully credentialed bunglers in this work, but that does not equate to saying that just anyone should set up shop to be a therapist. If one, no matter what her or his education, intends to offer psychotherapy, that person should in respect for human dignity seek preparation that is thorough and meaningful. This is not the place in which to give my views of that curriculum, but copies of a draft program that I have developed may be had by writing the Humanistic Psychology Institute, 325 Ninth Street, San Francisco, California 94103.

My Personal Experience of Being a Psychotherapist

My wife and I were just trying to decide whether to watch the 11 o'clock news when the phone rang. Late phone calls are seldom good news in a psychotherapist's life, and I picked the instrument up with misgivings. It was Sally. "Dr. Bugental, I've just stabbed my husband to death, and I don't know what I should do." Oh, God! It's happened. I've been so lucky, so seldom have my clients done truly violent acts, and now it's happened.

Meantime my voice is going on calmly, reasonably—mustn't panic her into doing anything else: "Tell me about it, Sally."

She sounds calm, but it's a kind of calm I don't feel good about. What's under the surface? "We argued again, just like always. I told him what I thought of him, and he said he was sick and tired of my moods. And then just as I told you . . . Oh, I haven't seen you lately to tell you, have I?"

"No, Sally, it's been a couple of months." Been trying to get her to come in regularly, and she keeps avoiding it. Now I know I should have insisted or told her I couldn't be available in this on-again off-again basis. Boy, all these hindsight and self-defensive thoughts! I'm scared, I'd better know that. "Sally, tell me where you are right now." Stalling while I try to think what to do. Got to keep touch with her, keep her from doing anything else or going anywhere.

"I'm just standing here looking at him."

"Are you sure he's dead?"

"Oh, he's dead all right." Little laugh. Is the control breaking? "What should I do, Dr. Bugental?"

"We've got to tell the police. You know that, don't you, Sally?"

"I suppose so."

"Do you want to do it, or do you want me to?"

"You do it."

"All right, Sally, I will, but I want you to promise me you'll just stay right there and not do anything else until I call you or the police come. Will you promise?"

"I promise."

And so we hang up, and I call the police and tell them what Sally has told me and ask them to call me as soon as they are with her and let me know whether I should come. That's ducking going there, I know it. I don't want to go there, and she hasn't asked me to.

An interminable half hour later the phone rings again. It's a police officer at Sally's house. "Doctor, we've been talking to this lady and her husband . . . !"

Sally had hallucinated the whole thing. No murder, no blood shed. Her husband took her to a hospital that very night, and I didn't hear from her for several months. When I did she was under the care of a psychiatrist whom her husband chose, and I was relieved of any further part in Sally's life.

I didn't make it with Sally, didn't help her make a commitment to psychotherapy. She would come three or four times and then miss appointments and say she would return later. By the book, I should have terminated her and refused to see her again. But I can't just do that to someone who is clearly reaching out for help but is so frightened of it at the same time. Others, given a chance to begin at their own pace, make it; Sally did not. Hindsight suggests so many things I could have done, but . . .

Sometimes the things clients say bring smiles and laughter to one or both of us. Not laughter *at* the client, but laughter of recognition at the marvelous humor and poetry of the larger self speaking through the client.

Gina expressed such a basic human truth once when I asked her, "Gina, what would it be like if you weren't frightened in any way?"

"Oh, gee, Jim, that would be pretty scary!"

Ted's mistrust showed through so clearly in a slip of speech when he told me, "I just knew I was going to die or have a prolonged, malingering kind of illness."

Betty reflected on a disappointment in a friend, "It kind of shattered my trust, a little bit." And another time she remarked, "I didn't even hear about the population explosion until I had five children!"

Pete expressed feelings not unlike Gina's when he told me soberly, "I'm still not comfortable with being happy."

And Carol invented a facility many of us could appreciate, "There ought to be a screamatorium where I could run down long corridors and scream and scream."

The generation gap was neatly expressed by Sarah when she avowed, "I want to go to Paris. It will kill my parents, but they'll survive." It was also Sarah who said, "My family always has given a lot of attention to their clothes, the way they dress. But I dress just anyway—well, no, not just anyway, in a very special way. I kind of anti-dress."

Psychotherapists have privileged seats at the enthralling pageant of human life. In time all moods, all emotions, all dramas are played out before them. But, if they are of the orientation I've been describing in this book, they cannot remain just spectators. Again and again, they are drawn into the action, and often that action reaches into their supposedly private lives to exert its claims on them. There is no tally of the interruptions made by client needs of conversations, fights, lovemaking, planning, and just quiet evenings. At first this being on call seemed glamorous and a demonstration of one's importance. But it didn't take many such interruptions to learn that I must protect some time if I was to be truly available at other times. Now, explicitly and implicitly, I invite calls much less, and I give myself periods of protection from any intrusion.

Some personal reflections

I am not the person who began to practice counseling or psychotherapy more than 30 years ago in an army hospital. And the changes in me are not solely those worked by time, education, and the life circumstances shared by most of my generation. A powerful force affecting me has been my participation in so many lives. A psychotherapist had best recognize that the profession will continually press on her or him to change and evolve. Those sad doctors that Rogow (1970) describes, who are so bored with their work, must surely have armored themselves against the insistent confrontations of intimate contact with human lives. This work is exciting, constantly changing, demanding, exhausting, frightening, stimulating, dangerous, socially borderline, culturally essential, and much else—but the one thing it is not is boring!

Speaking simply as one person, my life as a psychotherapist has brought me a good income, a modicum of prestige and success, and a feeling of belonging to an honorable community and profession. It has injected me into many rich, exciting, and sometimes frightening relationships. It has given me an arena for my creativity and endless raw materials to feed it. It has been the source of anguish, pain, and anxiety—sometimes in the work itself, but more frequently within myself and with those important in my life in confrontations stimulated directly or indirectly by the impact of the work and the relationships with my clients. Similarly that work and those relationships have directly and indirectly brought to me and those in my life joy, excitement, and a sense of participation in truly vital experiences. Because of the insistent impetus to grow, to change, to open up new possibilities, and to keep in touch with my own inner self, my life has gone through several major revisions. I doubt I would have chosen these otherwise, but I feel the more realized for having hung on through them, and I look with anticipation and apprehension to what may lie ahead, for I feel still that surge of continual change within me.

Finally, and in some ways most importantly, being a psychotherapist has meant having a window on the human soul. Such a hard thing to try to say what that means. For me it has been acutely, poignantly important. It has given me what I think I always lacked before: a ground on which to stand in being alive, a foundation upon which to build an outlook for my own life and on life and death as our common heritage and fate. I believe in my deepest heart that I have realized more of my possibilities through this life than I could have in any other way. And I am grateful.

References

Allport, G. W. *Personality: A Psychological Interpretation.* New York: Holt, 1937.

Balsam, R. M. and Balsam, A. *Becoming a Psychotherapist: A Clinical Primer.* Boston: Little, Brown, 1974.

Bockoven, J. S. *Moral Treatment in American Psychiatry.* New York: Springer, 1963.

Brammer, L. M. and Shostrom, E. L. *Therapeutic Psychology: Fundamentals of Actualization Counseling and Psychotherapy* (2nd ed.). Englewood Cliffs, N.J.: Prentice-Hall, 1968.

Bruch, H. *Learning Psychotherapy: Rationale and Ground Rules.* Cambridge, Mass.: Harvard University Press, 1974.

Bugental, J. F. T. "A method for assessing self and not-self attitudes during the therapeutic series." *Journal of Consulting Psychology* 16 (1952): 435–439.

Bugental, J. F. T. *The Search for Authenticity: An Existential-analytic Approach to Psychotherapy.* New York: Holt, Rinehart, and Winston, 1965.

Bugental, J. F. T. "Commitment and the psychotherapist." *Existential Psychiatry* 6 (Whole No. 23): 285–292, 1967. (a)

Bugental, J. F. T. "The elastic clock." *Humanitas* 3 (1967): 5–21. (b)

Bugental, J. F. T. "The existential and the everyday." *American Journal of Orthopsychiatry* 37 (1967): 628–630. (c)

Bugental, J. F. T. "Psychotherapy as a source of the therapist's own authenticity and inauthenticity." *Voices* 4 (1968): 13–23.

Bugental, J. F. T. "Changes in inner human experience and the future." In

C. S. Wallia (Ed.), *Toward Century 21: Technology, Society, and Human Values.* New York: Basic Books, 1970, pp. 283–295.

Bugental, J. F. T. "The humanistic ethic: The individual in psychotherapy as a societal change agent." *Journal of Humanistic Psychology* 7 (1971): 11–25. (a)

Bugental, J. F. T. *The Human Possibility: An Essay Toward a Psychological Response to the World Macroproblems.* (Educational Policy Research Center, Research Memoradum EPRC 6747-16 Menlo Park, Calif.: Stanford Research Institute, 1971 (copyright, the author, 1974). (b)

Bugental, J. F. T. "The flight from finitude: Sadism, exhibitionism, and political madness. *Voices* 10 (1974): 40–46.

Bugental, J. F. T. "Toward a subjective psychology: Tribute to Charlotte Buhler." *Interpersonal Development* 6 (1975/76): (1), 55–66.

Bugental, J. F. T. *The Search for Existential Identity: Patient-therapist Dialogues in Humanistic Psychotherapy.* San Francisco: Jossey-Bass, 1976.

Burton, A. *Modern Humanistic Psychotherapy.* San Francisco: Jossey-Bass, 1967.

Castaneda, C. *The Teachings of Don Juan: A Yaqui Way of Knowledge.* New York: Ballentine, 1968.

Castaneda, C. *A Separate Reality: Further Conversations with Don Juan.* New York: Touchstone, 1971.

Castaneda, C. *Journey to Ixtlan: The Lessons of Don Juan.* New York: Simon and Schuster, 1972.

Castaneda, C. *Tales of Power.* New York: Simon and Schuster, 1974.

Cogswell, J. F. "An experience in conflict between the self and technology." In B. Marshall (Ed.) *Experience in Being.* Belmont, Calif.: Brooks/Cole, 1971, pp. 246–253.

Cogswell, J. F. Personal communication, January 11, 1977.

Colby, K. *A Primer for Psychotherapists.* New York: Ronald Press, 1951.

Deikman, A. *Personal Freedom: On Finding Your Way to the Real World.* New York: Grossman, 1976.

Farber, L. H. *The Ways of the Will: Essays Toward a Psychology and Psychopathology of Will.* New York: Basic Books, 1966.

Fierman, L. B. (Ed.). *Effective Psychotherapy: The Contribution of Hellmuth Kaiser.* New York: Free Press, 1965.

Friedman, M. *To Deny Our Nothingness: Contemporary Images of Man.* New York: Delacorte, 1967.

Fromm-Reichmann, F. *Principles of Intensive Psychotherapy.* Chicago: University of Chicago Press, 1950.

Gendlin, E. T. *Experiencing and the Creation of Meaning: A Philosophical and Psychological Approach to the Subjective.* Glencoe, IL: The Free Press of Glencoe, 1962.

Hammer, M. "Quiet mind therapy." *Voices* 7 (1971): (1 Whole No. 23) 52–56.

Horney K. *Neurosis and Human Growth.* New York: Norton, 1950.

Kübler-Ross, E. *On Death and Dying.* New York: Macmillan, 1969.

Lilly, J. C. *The Center of the Cyclone: An Autobiography of Inner Space.* New York: Julian Press, 1972.

Maslow, A. H. "Self-actualization and beyond." In J. F. T. Bugental (Ed.), *Challenges of Humanistic Psychology.* New York: McGraw-Hill, 1967.

Maslow, A. H. *Toward a Psychology of Being* (2nd ed.). New York: Van Nostrand Reinhold, 1968.

Maslow, A. H. *The Farther Reaches of Human Nature.* New York: Viking, 1971.

May, R. *Love and Will.* New York: Norton, 1969. (a)

May, R. "William James' humanism and the problem of will." In R. B. MacLeod (Ed.), *William James: Unfinished Business.* Washington, D.C.: American Psychological Association, 1969, pp. 73–91. (b)

McGlashan, A. *The Savage and Beautiful Country.* Boston: Houghton Mifflin, 1967.

Mischlov, J. *The Roots of Consciousness.* New York: Random House, 1975.

Moody, R. A., Jr. *Life After Life: The Investigation of a Phenomenon—Survival of Bodily Death.* Atlanta: Mockingbird, 1975.

Novak, M. *The Experience of Nothingness.* New York: Harper & Row, 1970.

Raimy, V. C. "Self-reference in counseling interviews." *Journal of Consulting Psychology* 12 (1948): 153–163.

Ram Dass, *The Only Dance There Is.* Garden City, NY: Anchor Books, 1974.

Reich, W. *Character Analysis.* New York: Orgone Institute Press, 1949.

Rogers, C. R. *Counseling and Psychotherapy: Newer Concepts in Practice.* Boston: Houghton Mifflin, 1942.

Rogers, C. R. *Client-centered Therapy: Its Current Practice, Implications, and Theory.* Boston: Houghton Mifflin, 1951.

Rogers, C. R. *On Becoming a Person.* Boston: Houghton Mifflin, 1961.

Rogow, A. A. *The Psychiatrists.* New York: G. P. Putnam's Sons, 1970.

Samuels, M. and Samuels, N. *Seeing with the Mind's eye: History, Technique, and Uses of Visualization.* New York: Random House, 1975.

Saul, I. J. *Technic and Practice of Psychoanalysis.* Philadelphia: Lippincott, 1958.

Sullivan, H. S. *Conceptions of Modern Psychiatry.* New York: Norton, 1947.

Van Dusen, W. *The Natural Depth in Man.* New York: Harper and Row, 1972.

Walsh, R. N. "Reflections on psychotherapy." *Journal of Transpersonal Psychology* **8** (1976): (2), 100–111.

Suggested Readings

Some representative literature is listed below for the aid of the reader who wishes to explore further the fields dealt with in this text. There is, of course, a voluminous body of writings, and this list does not try to do more than suggest starting points for further reading.

Background in Humanistic Psychology

Bugental, J. F. T. (Ed.). *Challenges of Humanistic Psychology.* New York: McGraw-Hill, 1967.

Dubos, R. *Beast or Angel? Choices that Make Us Human.* New York: Scribner's, 1974.

Gendlin, E. T. *Experiencing and the Creation of Meaning: A Philosophical and Psychological Approach to the Subjective.* Glencoe, Il: Free Press, 1962.

Kinget, G. M. *On Being Human: A Systematic View.* New York: Harcourt Brace Jovanovich, 1975.

Maslow, A. H. *The Farther Reaches of Human Nature.* New York: Viking, 1971.

Rogers, C. R. *On Becoming a Person.* Boston: Houghton Mifflin, 1961.

Background for Existential Perspective

Greening, T. C. (Ed.). *Existential-humanistic Psychology.* Belmont, Calif.: Brooks/Cole, 1971.

Koestenbaum, P. *The Vitality of Death: Essays in Existential Psychology and Philosophy.* Westport, CT: Greenwood, 1971.

May, R. *Love and Will.* New York: Norton, 1972.

Novak, M. *The Experience of Nothingness.* New York: Harper and Row, 1970.

Tillich, P. *The Courage to Be.* New Haven: Yale University Press, 1952.

Psychotherapeutic Metapsychology

Burton, A. *Modern Humanistic Psychotherapy.* San Francisco: Jossey-Bass, 1967.

Farber, L. H. *The Ways of the Will. Essays Toward a Psychology and Psychopathology of Will.* New York: Basic Books, 1966.

Fierman, L. B. (Ed.). *Effective Psychotherapy: The Contribution of Hellmuth Kaiser.* New York: Free Press, 1965.

Horney, K. *Neurosis and Human Growth: The Struggle Toward Self-realization.* New York: Norton, 1950.

Reich, W. *Character Analysis.* New York: Orgone Institute Press, 1949. (Part One is especially important.)

Wheelis, A. *How People Change.* New York: Harper and Row, 1973.

Psychotherapeutic Procedure and Perspective

Argelander, H. *The Initial Interview in Psychotherapy.* (H. F. Bernays, trans.). New York: Human Sciences Press, 1976.

Bruch, H. *Learning Psychotherapy: Rationale and Ground Rules.* Cambridge, Mass.: Harvard University Press, 1974.

Bugental, J. F. T. *The Search for Authenticity: An Existential-analytic Approach to Psychotherapy.* New York: Holt, Rinehart and Winston, 1965.

Bugental, J. F. T. *The Search for Existential Identity: Patient-therapist Dialogues in Humanistic Psychotherapy.* San Francisco: Jossey-Bass, 1976.

Fromm-Reichmann, F. *Principles of Intensive Psychotherapy.* Chicago: University of Chicago Press, 1950.

Kelman, H. *The Process in Psychoanalysis: A Manual.* New York: American Institute of Psychoanalysis, 1948/63.

May, R., Angel, E., and Elllensberger, H. F. (Eds.). *Existence: A New Dimension in Psychiatry and Psychology.* New York: Basic Books, 1958.

Saul, L. J. *Technic and Practice of Psychoanalysis.* Philadelphia: Lippincott, 1958.

The Further Vision

Castaneda, C. *Tales of Power.* New York: Simon and Schuster, 1974.

Deikman, A. *Personal Freedom: On Finding Your Way to the Real World.* New York: Grossman, 1976.

Needleman, J. *A Sense of the Cosmos: The Encounter of Modern Science and Ancient Truth.* Garden City, NY: Doubleday, 1975.

Ram Dass. *The Only Dance There Is.* Garden City, NY: Anchor Books, 1974.

Van Dusen, W. *The Natural Depth in Man.* New York: Harper and Row, 1972.

Index